Statistics of Alcohol Use and Alcoholism in Canada, 1871-1956

FIRST
REPORT

STATISTICS OF ALCOHOL USE AND ALCOHOLISM IN CANADA 1871-1956

COMPILED BY

Robert E. Popham & Wolfgang Schmidt

WITH THE ASSISTANCE OF

R. G. WILLIAMS
JEAN BRONETTO
C. P. COOPER

FOREWORD BY

John R. Seeley

UNIVERSITY OF
TORONTO PRESS

ALCOHOLISM
RESEARCH FOUNDATION

Foreword

THIS volume marks the formalization of an enterprise which the Alcoholism Research Foundation of Ontario has long carried on: the supplying of statistics, as reliable and extensive as they can currently be made, upon those principal matters about which we are most frequently questioned.

The volume is on essentially the same footing as the national census: it carries no arguments, makes no pleas, presents its facts with a minimum of interpretation—and, even then, interpretation chiefly to make clear what the scientist may infer from the facts, rather than what the policy-maker may choose to regard them as meaning. It is a compilation, then, of facts open to all who hold varying views upon the problems of alcohol and alcohol-use, part of what we hope will be the common ground between them as they explore and pursue their differences. It is hoped that, in time, it will become the standard or authoritative reference work for Canada, over the domain of the matters it deals with.

In annual revisions it is hoped to bring the various series up to date, to extend reporting into matters not now covered, and, if we can find ways to do so, to increase the reliability of the figures reported and improve the methods of presentation. In the pursuit of these aims we would welcome suggestions from all serious users of the document.

Meanwhile, it is offered, both with modesty and pride, to general policy-makers, to those with specialized interests in alcohol, and to our colleagues in the sciences, pure and applied. We hope particularly that physicians, social workers, social scientists—and interested "laymen"—will find in it something of what they want.

JOHN R. SEELEY
Director of Research

Alcoholism Research Foundation
of Ontario

Introduction

THE number of requests for statistical information relating
to alcohol-use and alcoholism in Canada, which are received annually by the Alcoholism Research Foundation,
has grown steadily since its inception in 1951. These requests
come from all parts of the country, and from representatives
of a variety of groups, including: temperance societies, the
alcoholic beverage industries, government liquor enquiry com-
missions, public relations consultants, opinion survey organiza-
tions, industrial and military personnel, welfare agencies, physicians, provincial foundations, various philanthropic groups concerned with the treatment and rehabilitation of the alcoholic,
research-workers, teachers, alcohol information centres, and persons associated with such mass media of communication as the
newspaper, magazine, radio, and television.

In the past, this widespread demand has most often been
met on an individual basis: a time-consuming and frequently
repetitious process. Periodically, new data—especially the latest
estimates of alcoholism prevalence—have been released through
the press. However, the quantity of material which can be provided by this means is extremely limited, and it is seldom
possible to adequately control the manner in which it is ultimately presented to the public. In 1954 a first attempt was
made to bring together some of the more commonly requested
statistics in a single report, and, subsequently, a number of
articles containing additional data were published.* But these
sources are scattered, most are now in many respects out-of-
date, and all are relatively limited in scope. Accordingly, the

*See: Popham, R.E., A statistical report relating to alcoholism and the use of alcoholic
beverages in Canada (*Internat. J. Alcohol & Alcoholism* 1: 5-22, 1955), Alcoholism
admission trends analyzed (*Alcoholism Research*, 2 (4): 1-7, 1955), The Jellinek
alcoholism estimation formula and its application to Canadian data (*Quart. J. Stud.
on Alcohol*, 17: 559-593, 1956); and Gibbins, R. J., Alcoholism in Canada (*Canada's
Health & Welfare*, Feb. 1954, pp. 2-3), Do you wonder about alcohol? (*Health*, July-
Aug. 1954, pp. 10-11), The alcoholism problem in Canada (*Can. Welfare*, 31 (2):
111-113, 1955).

present volume was prepared as the first of an annual series which it is hoped will help to meet the evident need for comprehensive and regular reporting of Canadian alcohol statistics.

THE SCOPE OF THE REPORT

The scope of the report may be conveniently described from the point of view of geographic coverage, historical depth, and type of data provided. With respect to geographic coverage, data are included for all provinces, and for the country as a whole. Only the Yukon and Northwest Territories are excluded, since the available data are very incomplete. However, in future reports it may prove desirable to add certain tabulations for these areas, and also for smaller geographic units such as the county and city.

The period within which data were sought extended from 1871, the year of the First Census of Canada, to 1956, the latest year for which most types of data were available at the time of writing. However, vital statistics for years prior to 1901 are not included, owing to the fact that very few provinces published the figures required, and standards of reporting and diagnosis differed so greatly from those employed in later years that the available data were felt to be of dubious value. In addition, many other, sometimes large, gaps occur in the various tabulations. For example, no figures are shown for Newfoundland prior to its entry into the Confederation in 1949; alcohol consumption figures are not included for any province for the period from 1894 to the passing of provincial prohibition laws; vital statistics are tabulated for only four provinces prior to 1921; and a number of series are largely or entirely confined to the post-war decade. In the majority of cases the relevant data do not appear to have been reported in any published source. However, in a few instances, fuller utilization of various provincial government documents may provide the necessary data to fill or reduce certain of these gaps in future volumes of the series.

With the exception of the data concerning the size and characteristics of the drinking population (Part I), all of the statistics provided were obtained from official government reports, or were calculated on the basis of data so obtained. Statistics of attitudes, those of primarily local interest, and those which were available for only a limited portion of the country, such as certain clinical statistics compiled by alcoholism foundations, are not included. Attention was confined to statistical data regularly reported, and available for the whole or most of the Dominion.

Apart from the foregoing and one or two additional limitations, nearly all available types of statistical data, which seemed relevant on the basis of current research needs and the diverse enquiries which have been received, are included in the report. The principal exceptions were "outlet" statistics (i.e., numbers of licensed stores, taverns, clubs, etc.), which are not reported on a national basis but are available for periods of varying lengths in the reports of some provincial liquor boards. However, licensing regulations differ greatly from one province to another, and from one period to another in the same province. Accordingly, the rather formidable task of compiling comparable figures was postponed for future volumes.

The data are presented in four parts and comprise: statistics of users and abstainers (Part I), of apparent alcohol consumption (Part II), of judicial offences involving alcohol (Part III), and vital and other statistics relating to the prevalence of alcoholism (Part IV). In a fifth and final section, the population data, employed to calculate various rates, are provided. Parenthetically, certain "control" data are included in a number of tabulations in order to facilitate trend studies. Thus, when the significance of a particular trend is under consideration, it is usually desirable to compare it with a more general trend of the same class, for example, deaths from liver cirrhosis with deaths from all causes. For this purpose, certain economic data are provided in Part II, convictions for all types of offence in Part III, general mortality data, and mental hospital admissions for all causes in Part IV.

Within each section, and for each type of statistic, the usual procedure has been to provide: first, the primary data for Canada and provinces, by year; second, where applicable, equally detailed tabulations of the same data expressed in the form of rates; third, a summary table containing the latest figures by province; fourth, if possible, a tabulation of comparable data for other countries; and, finally, a series of notes containing the sources employed, and various comments on the data. A detailed and comprehensive exposition of the difficulties and pitfalls, to which the interpretation of alcohol statistics seems especially liable, is planned for future volumes. For the present, the reader's attention is directed to the section notes in which some of the principal factors to be taken into account are outlined.

Acknowledgments

Special thanks are due to the various members of the staff of the Dominion Bureau of Statistics, who have always patiently and fully answered our many enquiries, and supplied reports and various data, sometimes in advance of publication. Among these we would particularly like to mention: Messrs. W. Bluger, R. B. Crozier, F. Curry, W. A. Magill, H. G. Page, and D. L. Ralston. It should be stressed that neither these members of the staff, nor the Bureau as a whole, are in any respect responsible for errors, omissions, or other shortcomings which this report may have. Such responsibility lies solely with the compilers.

Grateful acknowledgment is also due to: the American and Canadian Institutes of Public Opinion for data included in Part I, as indicated in the notes to the latter; to Mr. A. P. W. Clarke, Chief Chemist of the Liquor Control Board of Ontario, for his comprehensive reply to our enquiries concerning the alcoholic content of beverages sold in Canada; to Mr. Elmo C. Wilson, President of International Research Associates Inc., for permission to reproduce the New York *Herald Tribune* World Poll data shown in Table I—5; and, finally, to our three assistants, whose names appear on the title page, for painstakingly and conscientiously undertaking, among other things, the often extremely monotonous task of repeatedly checking the data at all stages of calculation and compilation.

R.E.P.
W.S.

Toronto
July, 1958

WARNING TO THE READER

All alcoholism prevalence estimates in this report have been based on the widely accepted and still unimproved-upon Jellinek Estimation Formula. Since work-in-process in the Research Department of the Alcoholism Research Foundation has raised but not yet settled questions about the formula, all prevalence estimates should be regarded as most tentative. Later revisions may well show the same relative order in the estimates, but call for much higher absolute numbers in every case.

Contents

xiv

PART I

The Size and Characteristics of the Drinking Population

TABLE I—1

THE PROPORTION OF USERS OF ALCOHOLIC BEVERAGES, AND OF TOTAL ABSTAINERS
IN VARIOUS SEGMENTS OF THE ADULT POPULATION OF CANADA ACCORDING TO
CANADIAN INSTITUTE OF PUBLIC OPINION SURVEYS 1948-1955
(For sources and notes, see page 11.)

Population	No. of respondents	Users (%)	Abstainers (%)
A. 1948			
Canada	2,035	64	36
Region			
Maritimes	211	49	51
Quebec	543	64	36
Ontario	682	65	35
Prairies and B.C.	599	70	30
Sex			
Male	1,063	77	23
Female	972	51	49
Age			
21-29	420	66	34
30-49	1,039	70	30
50 and over	576	53	47
Size of community			
Farm	474	53	47
Under 10,000	605	65	35
10,000-100,000	383	68	32
Over 100,000	573	71	29
B. 1949			
Canada	2,075	65	35
Region			
Maritimes	224	56	44
Quebec	605	62	38
Ontario	634	66	34
Prairies and B.C.	612	68	32
Sex			
Male	1,055	75	25
Female	1,020	54	46
Age			
21-29	396	67	33
30-49	988	70	30
50 and over	691	56	44

TABLE I—1 (*continued*)

Population	No. of respondents	Users (%)	Abstainers (%)
B. 1949 (*continued*)			
Religious denomination			
Roman Catholic	806	64	36
United	460	61	39
Anglican	280	75	25
Other	436	61	39
No church	93	77	23
Education			
Primary or no schooling	972	58	42
Secondary or high	841	68	32
University	262	76	24
Size of community			
Farm	474	53	47
Under 10,000	583	62	38
10,000–100,000	425	72	28
Over 100,000	593	71	29
C. 1950			
Canada	1,766	67	33
Region			
Maritimes	192	47	53
Quebec	498	67	33
Ontario	546	70	30
Prairies and B.C.	530	73	27
Sex			
Male	888	79	21
Female	878	56	44
Age			
21–29	381	67	33
30–49	867	73	27
50 and over	518	59	41
Religious denomination			
Roman Catholic	644	69	31
United	393	59	41
Anglican	245	80	20
Other	431	65	35
No church	53	79	21

TABLE I—1 (continued)

Population	No. of respondents	Users (%)	Abstainers (%)
	D. 1951		
Canada	2,017	64	36
Region			
Maritimes	206	53	47
Quebec	550	65	35
Ontario	690	64	36
Prairies and B.C.	571	65	35
Sex			
Male	1,023	74	26
Female	994	54	46
Age			
21–29	342	67	33
30–49	1,023	71	29
50 and over	652	51	49
Religious denomination			
Roman Catholic	749	65	35
United	454	59	41
Anglican	261	75	25
Other	484	60	40
No church	69	71	29
	E. 1952		
Canada	1,689	70	30
Region			
Maritimes	193	59	41
Quebec	450	71	29
Ontario	570	69	31
Prairies and B.C.	476	75	25
Sex			
Male	839	76	24
Female	850	64	36
Age			
21–29	575	74	26
30–39	414	75	25
40–49	321	69	31
50 and over	379	59	41

5

TABLE I—1 (continued)

Population	No. of respondents	Users (%)	Abstainers (%)
E. 1952 (continued)			
Religious denomination			
Roman Catholic	—	71	29
Protestant	—	70	30
Education			
Less than high school	—	65	35
High school or more	—	73	27
Economic status			
Poor	—	66	34
Average	—	72	28
Prosperous	—	76	24
Size of community			
Farm	—	62	38
Under 10,000	—	67	33
10,000–100,000	—	72	28
Over 100,000	—	76	24
F. 1955			
Canada	1,887	72	28
Region			
Maritimes	196	57	43
Quebec	616	69	31
Ontario	596	71	29
Prairies and B.C.	479	81	19
Sex			
Male	973	81	19
Female	914	62	38
Age			
21–29	448	73	27
30–39	556	79	21
40–49	466	72	28
50 and over	417	61	39
Religious denomination			
Roman Catholic	726	73	27
Protestant	1,118	71	29
Education			
Primary or no schooling	734	67	33
Secondary or high	978	74	26
University	175	76	24

TABLE I—1 (*continued*)

Population	No. of respondents	Users (%)	Abstainers (%)
	F. 1955 (*continued*)		
Occupation			
Business and professional	386	76	24
Clerical and sales	499	71	29
Skilled and unskilled labour	612	72	28
Farmers	268	66	34
Other	122	71	29
Language			
French only	267	60	40
English only	1,267	73	27
French and English	333	76	24
Car ownership			
Own car	1,241	73	27
No car	646	69	31

TABLE I—2

THE PERCENTAGE OF USERS OF ALCOHOLIC BEVERAGES IN VARIOUS SEGMENTS OF THE ADULT POPULATION OF CANADA ACCORDING TO CANADIAN INSTITUTE OF PUBLIC OPINION SURVEYS, 1943–1955
(For sources and notes, see page 11.)

Population	1943	1945	1948	1949	1950	1951	1952	1955
Canada	59	64	64	65	67	64	70	72
Region								
Maritimes	—	—	49	56	47	53	59	57
Quebec	—	—	64	62	67	65	71	69
Ontario	—	—	65	66	70	64	69	71
Prairies and B.C.	—	—	70	68	73	65	75	81
Sex								
Male	72	—	77	75	79	74	76	81
Female	45	—	51	54	56	54	64	62
Age								
21–29	59	—	66	67	67	67	74	73
30–49	64	—	70	70	73	71	72	76
50 and over	53	—	53	56	59	51	59	61

TABLE I—2 (continued)

Population	1943	1945	1948	1949	1950	1951	1952	1955
Religious denomination								
Roman Catholic	—	—	—	64	69	65	71	73
Protestant	—	—	—	64	66	63	70	71
Education								
Less than high school	—	—	—	58	—	—	65	67
High school or more	—	—	—	70	—	—	73	74
Size of community								
Farm	—	—	53	53	—	—	62	—
Under 10,000	—	—	65	62	—	—	67	—
10,000–100,000	—	—	68	72	—	—	72	—
Over 100,000	—	—	71	71	—	—	76	—

TABLE I—3

ESTIMATES OF THE NUMBER OF USERS OF ALCOHOLIC BEVERAGES IN THOUSANDS OF PERSONS AGED 15 YEARS AND OLDER IN CANADA AND PROVINCES, 1943–1955
(For sources and notes, see page 11.)

	Canada			Maritimes	Quebec	Ontario	Prairies &
	Male	Female	Total				B.C.
1943	3,156	1,867	5,023	—	—	—	—
1945	—	—	5,584	—	—	—	—
1948	3,573	2,289	5,862	405	1,638	2,070	1,791
1949	3,612	2,525	6,137	590	1,616	2,140	1,761
1950	3,849	2,661	6,510	497	1,777	2,309	1,912
1951	3,634	2,609	6,243	557	1,749	2,149	1,719
1952	3,834	3,162	6,996	631	1,962	2,386	2,021
1955	4,311	3,247	7,558	641	2,031	2,596	2,298

TABLE I—4

THE PERCENTAGE OF USERS OF ALCOHOLIC BEVERAGES, AND OF TOTAL ABSTAINERS
IN CANADA AND THE UNITED STATES IN EACH SURVEY YEAR, AND IN VARIOUS
SEGMENTS OF THE ADULT POPULATION
(For sources and notes, see page 12.)

	Canada		United States	
	Users	Abstainers	Users	Abstainers
1943	59	41	—	—
1945	64	36	67	33
1946	—	—	67	33
1947	—	—	63	37
1948	64	36	—	—
1949	65	35	58	42
1950	67	33	60	40
1951	64	36	59	41
1952	70	30	60	40
1955	72	28	—	—
1956	—	—	60	40
1957	—	—	58	42
Sex (Canada, 1955; U.S., 1957)				
Male	81	19	67	33
Female	62	38	50	50
Age (Canada, 1955; U.S., 1957)				
21–29	73	27	64	36
30–49	76	24	62	38
50 and over	61	39	48	52
Education (Canada, 1955; U.S., 1957)				
Primary or grammar school	67	33	46	54
Secondary or high school	74	26	63	37
College or university	76	24	64	36

9

TABLE I—5

THE PERCENTAGE OF FREQUENT AND OCCASIONAL USERS OF ALCOHOLIC BEVERAGES, AND OF TOTAL ABSTAINERS IN THE ADULT POPULATION OF VARIOUS COUNTRIES ACCORDING TO THE NEW YORK *Herald Tribune* WORLD POLL, 1958
(For sources and notes, see page 12.)

Country	Users			Abstainers
	Total	Occasional	Frequent	
Austria	82	74	8	17
France	80	50	30	19
Germany	77	73	4	21
Italy	76	58	18	22
Great Britain	73	62	11	27
Norway	68	66	2	26
Sweden	64	61	3	34
Canada	61	56	5	38
Belgium	61	59	2	39
Mexico*	53	52	1	45
Brazil†	43	40	3	57
Japan	42	31	11	58

*Based on data for Mexico City only.
†Based on data for Rio de Janeiro and São Paulo only.

SOURCES AND NOTES

Table I—1, A-F

All figures, with the exception of certain of the breakdowns shown for 1952, were specially provided during May, 1958, by the Canadian Institute of Public Opinion, through the generous co-operation of Miss Byrne Hope Sanders, Director. The breakdowns by religious denomination, education, economic status, and size of community for the year 1952 were previously obtained from the same Institute, through the kindness of the former Director, Mr. Wilfred Sanders (see Popham, R. E., A statistical report relating to alcoholism and the use of alcoholic beverages in Canada, *Internat. J. on Alcohol & Alcoholism,* I, 1955, pp. 17, 20).

All proportions were calculated by Institute staff on the basis of responses obtained from stratified samples of the adult (aged 21 and older) population to the question: "Do you ever have occasion to use any alcoholic beverages such as liquor, wine, or beer, or are you a total abstainer?"

Table I—2

All figures were based on the data provided in Table I—1, A-F, except those shown for the years 1943–1945. The proportion of users and abstainers in Canada in each of the latter years, and the age breakdown for 1943 were obtained from the Canadian Institute of Public Opinion Press Release of February 4, 1950; the sex breakdown for 1943 was obtained from the Release of December 10, 1955. The proportions for these two years were based on data collected in the same manner as noted above for the years 1948–1955.

It should be noted that the figures shown for the proportion of Protestant users in the years 1949, 1950, and 1951 were based on data separately reported by the Institute for United, Anglican, and "Other." It was assumed, on the basis of information available for other years, that the latter category included primarily respondents of other Protestant denominations and only a negligible number of non-Protestants.

Table I—3

All figures were obtained through application of the proportions shown in Table I—2 to the appropriate estimates of population aged 15 and older provided in Table V—1, A-K. The figures for Canada are exclusive of the Yukon and Northwest Territories throughout, and of Newfoundland until 1949. Discrepancies between the sum of the figures for each survey region and the estimated total drinking population of Canada are due to rounding errors.

The proportions reported by the Canadian Institute of Public Opinion for the Maritime Provinces (see Table I—2) referred to the area comprising Prince Edward Island, Nova Scotia and New Brunswick. To obtain the estimates shown above for the Maritimes from 1949 to 1955, these proportions were assumed to hold for Newfoundland as well.

Particular note should be taken of the fact that the Canadian Institute of Public Opinion surveys were based entirely on samples of the population aged 21 and older. On the other hand, the estimates of number of users provided above were based in each case on the population aged 15 and older. The assumption that the same proportion of users obtained in the 15–20 age group as in the adult population may be questioned. However, the results of a number of studies conducted in the United

11

States, and of at least one Canadian survey, suggested that a sizable proportion of persons in the 15–20 age group would have responded affirmatively to the question employed in the Canadian Institute of Public Opinion surveys. Accordingly, it was felt that estimates based on the 15 and older population were likely to be subject to smaller errors than if based on the adult population alone.

Table I—4

For the source of the Canadian figures, see notes to Table I—2. The survey results for the United States were obtained from Public Opinion News Service, Release of March 5, 1958, by George Gallup, Director of the American Institute of Public Opinion. The same question and sampling procedures were employed in the American Institute surveys as in those of the affiliated Canadian Institute (see notes to Table I—1, A-F).

It should be carefully noted that the breakdowns by sex, age, and education shown for the two countries are not strictly comparable. Those for Canada apply to the year 1955, whereas those for the United States apply to the year 1957, the nearest for which similar data were available.

Table I—5

Figures were obtained through the kindness of Mr. Elmo C. Wilson, President of International Research Associates, the organization which conducted the survey on behalf of the New York *Herald Tribune* World Poll. Mr. Wilson pointed out that the World Poll surveys are "based on scientific samples of 600 to 2,000 persons in the countries polled, and all the interviewing is done by native representatives in the countries concerned" (personal communication of May 23, 1958). Percentages were calculated on the basis of response to the question: "Do you yourself have alcoholic drinks frequently, only occasionally, or not at all?"

Discrepancies between 100%, and the sum of figures in column one (% total users) and column four (% abstainers) represent the percentage of respondents who did not answer the question.

Since the question employed in this survey differed considerably from that employed in the various surveys of the Canadian and American Institute of Public Opinion, the results as regards percentage of users and abstainers are not comparable. This factor together with differences in the samples employed may account for the not inconsiderable difference in the figures obtained for Canada by the World Poll and by the Canadian Institute of Public Opinion (see Table I—4).

12

PART II

The Apparent Consumption of Alcoholic Beverages

TABLE II—1

	Beer*	Wine*	Spirits*	Total*	Total per capita of 15 years and older
			A. Newfoundland		
1953	39.4	7.0	60.7	107.1	.46
1954	107.3	7.3	62.9	177.5	.74
1955	116.4	7.4	67.6	191.4	.78
1956	125.8	7.6	68.2	201.6	.80
		B. Prince Edward Island			
1874	5.1	0.7	20.9	26.7	.44
1875	4.0	0.9	25.6	30.5	.49
1876	4.9	1.5	37.0	43.4	.69
1877	4.2	0.8	32.9	37.9	.60
1878	3.3	0.4	18.3	22.0	.34
1879	2.6	0.6	26.7	29.9	.46
1880	2.9	0.2	19.2	22.3	.34
1881	2.1	0.3	24.9	27.3	.41
1882	1.5	0.2	20.2	21.9	.33
1883	1.0	0.6	19.8	21.4	.32
1884	1.2	0.2	16.6	18.0	.27
1885	1.7	0.2	20.5	22.4	.33
1886	1.9	0.3	27.8	30.0	.44
1887	2.4	0.4	12.4	15.2	.22
1888	2.0	0.2	12.4	14.6	.21
1889	3.2	0.1	10.4	13.7	.20
1890	1.8	0.2	11.9	13.9	.20
1891	2.6	0.2	11.3	14.1	.21
1892	1.8	0.2	11.9	13.9	.20
1893	1.6	0.2	13.1	14.9	.22
1894–1956	—	—	—	—	—
		C. Nova Scotia			
1871	23.0	7.3	127.4	157.7	.67
1872	20.7	8.4	140.1	169.2	.71
1873	21.2	6.4	144.4	172.0	.70
1874	21.8	8.6	162.3	192.7	.78
1875	19.7	4.7	122.5	146.9	.58
1876	23.9	5.0	117.9	146.8	.58

*Figures represent thousands of imperial gallons of absolute alcohol.

TABLE II—1 (*continued*)

	Beer	Wine	Spirits	Total	Total per capita of 15 years and older
C. Nova Scotia (*continued*)					
1877	15.4	4.5	121.1	141.0	.55
1878	18.0	3.4	91.8	113.2	.43
1879	17.0	4.0	97.7	118.7	.45
1880	12.6	2.2	82.8	97.6	.36
1881	24.1	3.6	99.8	127.5	.47
1882	15.4	4.6	103.5	123.5	.45
1883	14.2	4.6	112.6	129.4	.47
1884	17.9	4.5	112.8	135.2	.48
1885	17.9	4.0	107.0	128.9	.46
1886	19.0	4.6	93.4	117.0	.41
1887	15.1	2.4	90.3	107.8	.38
1888	21.6	3.0	75.4	100.0	.35
1889	27.5	3.8	95.4	126.7	.44
1890	33.4	3.4	125.9	162.7	.56
1891	32.1	3.6	86.3	122.0	.42
1892	29.3	3.1	87.4	119.8	.41
1893	28.1	2.7	79.4	110.2	.38
1894–1930	—	—	—	—	—
1931	60.5	20.3	36.7	117.5	.34
1932	55.4	16.2	23.7	95.3	.27
1933	43.7	17.8	16.5	78.0	.22
1934	44.9	27.0	16.0	87.9	.24
1935*	52.9	37.7	29.1	119.7	—
1936	46.9	23.6	45.4	115.9	.31
1937	56.7	16.3	58.8	131.8	.34
1938	50.7	18.7	66.2	135.6	.35
1939	53.2	25.1	81.2	159.5	.40
1940	94.5	35.2	99.4	229.1	.57
1941	133.8	19.3	147.9	301.1	.74
1942	167.7	21.6	183.2	372.5	.89
1943	175.6	16.9	120.7	313.2	.73
1944	206.3	18.1	130.6	355.0	.82
1945	221.1	18.1	139.5	378.7	.87
1946	254.0	26.3	168.8	449.1	1.05
1947	222.5	28.1	161.8	412.4	.96
1948	213.6	27.4	159.8	400.8	.93
1949	224.0	27.5	161.8	413.3	.96
1950	213.0	29.8	152.6	395.4	.91
1951†	272.1	42.3	208.1	522.5	—
1952	208.0	39.3	162.2	409.5	.93
1953	231.6	43.8	173.1	448.5	1.01

*Fourteen-month period.   † Sixteen-month period.

TABLE II—1 (*continued*)

	Beer	Wine	Spirits	Total	Total per capita of 15 years and older
		C. Nova Scotia (*continued*)			
1954	231.1	44.0	181.4	456.5	1.02
1955	217.5	52.4	182.1	452.0	1.00
1956	215.0	57.0	190.8	462.8	1.01
		D. New Brunswick			
1871	8.8	5.9	149.0	163.7	.97
1872	10.9	6.0	155.8	172.7	1.00
1873	12.3	7.1	171.1	190.5	1.09
1874	10.5	9.5	173.6	193.6	1.09
1875	10.0	3.7	136.5	150.2	.83
1876	10.0	4.2	125.0	139.2	.76
1877	8.4	3.3	100.5	112.2	.60
1878	12.2	2.8	118.8	133.8	.71
1879	10.2	2.9	102.6	115.7	.61
1880	7.8	1.3	81.1	90.2	.46
1881	2.1	2.4	104.0	108.5	.55
1882	10.6	2.7	123.4	136.7	.69
1883	13.0	3.1	131.8	147.9	.75
1884	13.4	3.0	116.7	133.1	.67
1885	14.5	2.4	109.2	126.1	.63
1886	16.6	2.4	82.1	101.1	.51
1887	15.7	1.8	85.7	103.2	.52
1888	16.2	2.0	77.2	95.4	.47
1889	16.7	2.3	91.9	110.9	.55
1890	17.7	2.2	104.5	124.4	.62
1891	17.3	2.2	76.7	96.2	.48
1892	17.5	1.9	80.8	100.2	.49
1893	17.0	1.6	83.7	102.3	.50
1894–1946	—	—	—	—	—
1947	146.4	34.3	129.0	309.7	.95
1948	136.8	34.3	124.6	295.7	.89
1949	105.0	41.4	122.4	268.8	.80
1950–1954	—	—	—	—	—
1955	139.5	36.2	115.6	291.3	.83
1956	158.8	39.3	124.0	322.1	.89
		E. Quebec			
1871	124.4	67.6	705.5	897.5	1.30
1872	133.4	85.2	794.3	1,012.9	1.44
1873	150.4	74.8	801.8	1,027.4	1.43
1874	138.4	92.5	844.9	1,075.8	1.47
1875	142.3	59.2	640.2	841.8	1.14

TABLE II—1 (*continued*)

	Beer	Wine	Spirits	Total	Total per capita of 15 years and older
		E. Quebec (*continued*)			
1876	136.5	75.3	669.7	881.5	1.17
1877	134.5	42.4	603.8	780.7	1.02
1878	117.2	43.8	606.3	767.7	0.99
1879	104.6	45.6	581.0	731.2	0.93
1880	101.4	36.9	471.7	613.0	0.77
1881	117.0	52.9	671.7	841.6	1.04
1882	138.0	63.1	738.7	939.8	1.14
1883	137.3	68.2	828.2	1,033.6	1.24
1884	146.2	59.6	772.9	978.7	1.16
1885	139.8	55.4	745.8	941.0	1.11
1886	160.2	53.8	574.1	788.1	0.92
1887	189.6	51.3	650.0	890.9	1.03
1888	194.4	56.5	594.6	845.5	0.97
1889	192.1	55.9	701.6	949.6	1.08
1890	207.3	60.6	744.7	1,012.6	1.14
1891	215.5	60.2	605.3	881.0	0.98
1892	202.1	55.1	561.4	818.6	0.90
1893	192.1	53.9	626.3	872.3	0.95
1894–1927	—	—	—	—	—
1928	1,431.6	229.4	391.7	2,052.7	1.19
1929	1,450.8	257.8	423.5	2,132.1	1.20
1930	1,496.8	259.3	428.5	2,184.6	1.20
1931	1,448.4	216.2	372.3	2,036.9	1.10
1932	1,294.8	181.1	297.7	1,773.6	0.93
1933	1,006.6	137.1	216.7	1,360.4	0.70
1934	943.7	135.1	209.5	1,288.3	0.65
1935	972.2	156.8	222.7	1,351.7	0.68
1936	969.2	151.8	344.9	1,465.9	0.72
1937	1,006.4	132.2	419.3	1,557.9	0.75
1938	1,150.6	134.9	500.0	1,785.5	0.84
1939	1,115.6	133.7	497.8	1,747.1	0.80
1940	1,066.7	170.4	413.2	1,650.3	0.74
1941*	1,103.6	193.4	420.1	1,717.1	—
1942	1,354.6	195.4	545.0	2,095.0	0.90
1943	1,550.2	236.1	642.0	2,428.3	1.03
1944	1,408.8	164.2	663.7	2,236.7	0.93
1945	1,612.3	200.8	771.0	2,584.1	1.06
1946	1,769.4	200.3	805.6	2,775.3	1.12
1947	1,910.4	264.9	947.6	3,122.9	1.24
1948	2,275.5	205.3	868.6	3,349.4	1.31
1949	2,544.1	174.9	819.5	3,538.5	1.36
1950	2,692.0	170.2	809.6	3,671.8	1.38

*Eleven-month period only.

TABLE II—1 (*continued*)

	Beer	Wine	Spirits	Total	Total per capita of 15 years and older
		E. Quebec (*continued*)			
1951	2,664.4	187.3	868.9	3,720.6	1.38
1952	2,760.5	203.0	870.4	3,833.9	1.39
1953	3,043.8	224.4	942.8	4,211.0	1.49
1954	3,101.7	236.8	964.9	4,303.4	1.49
1955	2,422.8	252.5	984.0	3,659.3	1.24
1956	3,170.9	267.8	1,083.1	4,521.8	1.50
		F. Ontario			
1871	209.0	14.8	989.9	1,213.7	1.30
1872	247.3	21.6	1,088.7	1,357.6	1.41
1873	294.2	25.2	1,037.3	1,356.7	1.37
1874	286.4	27.7	1,403.8	1,717.9	1.69
1875	318.0	17.3	929.7	1,265.0	1.22
1876	296.2	18.0	1,028.2	1,342.4	1.26
1877	282.5	8.5	773.2	1,064.2	.98
1878	271.1	6.0	775.4	1,052.5	.95
1879	299.7	8.8	1,103.0	1,411.5	1.24
1880	322.4	5.3	564.3	892.0	.77
1881	339.5	8.1	773.7	1,121.3	.94
1882	416.4	9.7	850.5	1,276.6	1.05
1883	448.6	12.1	920.2	1,380.9	1.12
1884	457.5	9.6	859.9	1,327.0	1.06
1885	410.9	9.3	1,176.7	1,596.9	1.26
1886	442.6	7.1	588.9	1,038.6	.81
1887	485.4	6.7	624.6	1,116.7	.86
1888	526.4	7.7	541.1	1,075.2	.81
1889	535.0	9.1	690.2	1,234.3	.92
1890	570.8	12.0	860.1	1,442.9	1.06
1891	584.7	10.8	636.1	1,231.6	.89
1892	542.5	9.1	571.9	1,123.5	.81
1893	557.9	8.6	623.5	1,190.0	.85
1894–1931	—	—	—	—	—
1932	430.6	295.8	400.3	1,126.7	.45
1933	374.6	271.8	350.1	996.5	.39
1934	595.7	224.3	357.8	1,177.8	.46
1935	804.0	232.7	364.1	1,400.8	.53
1936	1,082.3	204.2	513.5	1,800.0	.67
1937	1,165.9	236.8	599.6	2,002.3	.74
1938	1,291.1	261.7	673.9	2,226.7	.81
1939	1,236.9	274.7	670.4	2,182.0	.78
1940	1,367.5	291.6	597.5	2,256.6	.80
1941	1,535.8	325.8	653.9	2,515.5	.88

TABLE II—1 (*continued*)

	Beer	Wine	Spirits	Total	Total per capita of 15 years and older
F. Ontario (*continued*)					
1942	1,925.6	308.1	821.8	3,055.5	1.04
1943	2,080.9	334.3	796.6	3,211.8	1.08
1944	1,925.4	246.6	776.6	2,948.6	.98
1945	2,359.1	259.9	607.2	3,226.2	1.07
1946	2,552.5	342.2	1,064.4	3,959.1	1.28
1947	2,945.4	355.7	1,196.1	4,497.2	1.43
1948	3,408.1	375.3	1,186.6	4,970.0	1.56
1949	3,479.3	362.9	1,297.9	5,140.1	1.58
1950	3,499.9	359.3	1,399.7	5,258.9	1.59
1951	3,490.3	362.0	1,495.8	5,348.1	1.59
1952	3,733.3	331.4	1,503.0	5,567.7	1.61
1953	4,016.4	323.3	1,606.0	5,945.7	1.69
1954	4,180.2	327.0	1,684.8	6,192.0	1.72
1955	4,099.1	341.4	1,726.2	6,166.7	1.69
1956	4,375.2	351.2	1,869.8	6,596.2	1.78
G. Manitoba					
1871	.01	.4	6.2	6.6	.44
1872	.3	1.3	12.6	14.2	.84
1873	.1	1.3	22.1	23.5	1.18
1874	1.8	.4	4.2	6.4	.29
1875	1.9	.5	8.7	11.1	.44
1876	2.2	1.0	12.5	15.7	.58
1877	1.5	.1	6.4	8.0	.28
1878	3.6	.4	11.2	15.2	.51
1879	4.5	.5	18.8	23.8	.72
1880	6.0	.4	16.9	23.3	.67
1881	8.7	.5	25.7	34.9	.92
1882	14.9	2.0	45.6	62.5	1.42
1883	22.1	2.4	56.5	81.0	1.65
1884	19.6	1.2	51.8	72.6	1.32
1885	16.1	1.3	51.3	68.7	1.13
1886	19.6	1.5	48.1	69.2	1.05
1887	23.6	1.4	55.5	80.5	1.12
1888	24.6	1.6	34.6	60.8	.79
1889	27.5	1.8	46.8	76.1	.92
1890	11.8	1.5	51.4	64.7	.74
1891	28.7	1.2	53.4	83.3	.89
1892	26.6	1.8	66.3	94.7	.95
1893	28.9	1.9	71.3	102.1	.96
1894–1933	—	—	—	—	—
1934	105.1	22.8	32.9	160.8	.32
1935	109.4	20.7	50.4	180.5	.36

TABLE II—1 (*continued*)

	Beer	Wine	Spirits	Total	Total per capita of 15 years and older
G. Manitoba (*continued*)					
1936	112.2	20.3	66.1	198.6	.39
1937	121.3	23.4	79.6	224.3	.43
1938	141.1	24.0	82.5	247.6	.47
1939	141.2	25.2	81.4	247.8	.46
1940	156.1	29.9	82.9	268.9	.50
1941	197.9	31.1	96.8	325.8	.60
1942	212.2	36.5	117.6	366.3	.68
1943	218.3	39.5	109.4	367.2	.68
1944	240.3	27.2	85.9	353.4	.65
1945	338.6	28.2	85.8	452.6	.84
1946	338.6	31.1	130.8	500.5	.94
1947*	392.1	39.3	144.4	575.8	—
1948	429.1	39.7	152.0	620.8	1.14
1949	437.6	39.1	165.4	642.1	1.17
1950	451.3	39.7	181.1	672.1	1.22
1951	431.6	43.9	190.2	665.7	1.20
1952	443.8	44.0	199.0	686.8	1.22
1953	488.2	43.8	214.7	746.7	1.31
1954	502.2	42.4	221.8	766.4	1.32
1955	457.3	42.0	218.1	717.4	1.21
1956	514.1	41.6	224.9	780.6	1.31
H. Saskatchewan					
1943	143.3	54.7	79.4	277.4	.47
1944	161.0	41.7	75.6	278.3	.47
1945	192.7	40.3	65.9	298.9	.50
1946	293.2	42.2	101.2	436.6	.74
1947	268.0	65.1	123.8	456.9	.77
1948	365.8	53.7	115.2	534.7	.90
1949	384.7	42.0	129.2	555.9	.95
1950	395.2	45.8	148.8	589.8	1.02
1951	370.0	47.5	146.6	564.1	.98
1952	399.4	50.9	165.9	616.2	1.06
1953	466.6	52.3	195.6	714.5	1.20
1954	496.3	50.0	205.4	751.7	1.25
1955	444.0	50.4	211.6	706.0	1.17
1956	436.0	49.2	203.4	688.6	1.13
I. Alberta					
1928	228.3	27.5	86.3	342.1	.79
1929	220.0	35.2	87.2	342.4	.75

*Eleven-month period only.

23340

TABLE II—1 (*continued*)

	Beer	Wine	Spirits	Total	Total per capita of 15 years and older
		I. Alberta (*continued*)			
1930	213.9	32.5	85.3	331.7	.70
1931	177.1	26.1	64.5	267.7	.54
1932	143.1	23.0	47.9	214.0	.43
1933	130.2	16.2	37.2	183.6	.36
1934	126.8	16.2	38.2	181.2	.35
1935	146.8	20.3	47.0	214.1	.40
1936	151.6	20.3	47.0	218.9	.41
1937	150.0	18.4	90.8	259.2	.47
1938	157.4	17.4	45.1	219.9	.40
1939	164.3	17.2	107.0	288.5	.52
1940	179.8	20.6	93.9	294.3	.52
1941	201.7	20.6	97.6	319.9	.56
1942	245.9	22.1	113.4	381.4	.69
1943	285.1	28.6	123.4	437.1	.78
1944	280.0	20.2	94.9	395.1	.68
1945	362.7	22.1	146.4	531.2	.92
1946	466.3	20.8	138.5	625.6	1.09
1947	545.0	44.0	164.6	753.6	1.29
1948	555.2	49.6	167.7	772.5	1.29
1949	586.4	28.0	196.8	811.2	1.31
1950	619.7	31.7	221.3	872.7	1.37
1951	607.2	37.2	235.1	879.5	1.35
1952	633.5	42.0	261.9	937.4	1.40
1953	700.1	47.1	309.4	1,056.6	1.54
1954	715.5	50.0	333.2	1,098.7	1.56
1955	676.6	54.1	336.7	1,067.4	1.49
1956	688.9	57.6	359.7	1,106.2	1.53
		J. British Columbia			
1872	.9	2.5	14.1	17.5	.67
1873	1.2	2.1	19.7	23.0	.85
1874	5.6	2.2	23.7	31.5	1.13
1875	9.3	3.2	24.5	37.0	1.28
1876	8.7	3.2	27.7	39.6	1.32
1877	7.5	2.9	23.8	34.2	1.10
1878	7.6	2.9	26.8	37.3	1.17
1879	7.5	3.4	34.9	45.8	1.39
1880	7.1	2.9	19.4	29.4	.86
1881	8.1	4.1	26.7	38.9	1.11
1882	8.2	5.6	29.3	43.1	1.11
1883	10.5	6.8	34.5	51.8	1.21
1884	13.2	7.4	34.1	54.7	1.19
1885	14.5	8.8	42.2	65.5	1.31

TABLE II—1 (*continued*)

	Beer	Wine	Spirits	Total	Total per capita of 15 years and older
		J. British Columbia (*continued*)			
1886	15.8	8.3	40.6	64.7	1.20
1887	17.5	8.3	35.2	61.0	1.07
1888	20.8	3.9	42.3	67.0	1.10
1889	25.8	5.4	53.3	84.5	1.30
1890	29.2	7.5	65.7	102.4	1.48
1891	34.3	7.9	60.9	103.1	1.41
1892	39.5	8.1	71.4	119.0	1.51
1893	39.1	7.6	68.8	115.5	1.36
1894–1952	–	–	–	–	–
1953	725.9	60.5	617.8	1,404.2	1.58
1954	708.4	68.4	619.1	1,395.9	1.53
1955	720.3	78.3	625.4	1,424.0	1.53
1956	783.2	82.3	678.9	1,544.4	1.62

TABLE II—2

THE PERCENTAGE CONTRIBUTION OF BEER, WINE, AND SPIRITS TO THE APPARENT
TOTAL CONSUMPTION OF ABSOLUTE ALCOHOL, AND TOTAL ALCOHOL CONSUMPTION
PER CAPITA IN CANADA, 1871–1956
(For sources and notes, see page 32.)

	Beer	Wine	Spirits	Total per capita of 15 years and older
1871	15	4	81	1.19
1872	15	5	80	1.29
1873	17	4	79	1.29
1874	15	4	81	1.42
1875	20	4	76	1.07
1876	19	4	77	1.10
1877	21	3	76	0.90
1878	20	3	77	0.87
1879	18	3	79	0.99
1880	26	3	71	0.69
1881	22	3	75	0.88
1882	23	3.5	73.5	0.98
1883	23	3	74	1.06
1884	25	3	72	0.99
1885	21	3	76	1.06
1886	30.5	3.5	66	0.78

TABLE II—2 *(continued)*

	Beer	Wine	Spirits	Total per capita of 15 years and older
1887	31.5	3	65.5	0.83
1888	36	3	61	0.78
1889	32	3	65	0.89
1890	30	3	67	0.98
1891	36	3.5	60.5	0.84
1892	36	3	61	0.78
1893	34.5	3	62.5	0.81
1894–1921	—	—	—	—
1922	59	4	37	0.54
1923	60	5	35	0.50
1924	59.5	7	33.5	0.57
1925	63	7	30	0.58
1926	64	8	28	0.62
1927	56	9	31	0.62
1928	54	10	36	0.77
1929	53.5	10.5	36	0.85
1930	52	13	35	0.87
1931	54.5	13.5	32	0.76
1932	56	14	30	0.65
1933	60	15	25	0.46
1934	59	15	26	0.46
1935	62	14	24	0.56
1936	59	10	31	0.63
1937	57	10	33	0.67
1938	56.5	10	33.5	0.74
1939	55.5	10	34.5	0.70
1940	54	10	36	0.74
1941	58	11	31	0.82
1942	58.5	8.5	33	0.91
1943	59	9	32	0.98
1944	64	8	28	0.82
1945	67	7	26	0.94
1946	61	7	32	1.20
1947	61.5	7.5	31	1.33
1948	62.5	6.5	31	1.46
1949	65	6	29	1.41
1950	65.5	5.5	29	1.44
1951	62	6	32	1.47
1952	64	6	30	1.46
1953	66.5	5.5	28	1.44
1954	66.5	5.5	28	1.46
1955	63.5	6.5	30	1.39
1956	64.5	5.5	30	1.51

TABLE II—3

THE PERCENTAGE CONTRIBUTION OF BEER, WINE, AND SPIRITS TO THE APPARENT
TOTAL CONSUMPTION OF ABSOLUTE ALCOHOL, AND TOTAL ALCOHOL CONSUMPTION
PER CAPITA IN CANADA AND PROVINCES, 1956

(For sources and notes, see page 33.)

Area	Beer	Wine	Spirits	Total per capita of 15 years and older
Canada	64.5	5.5	30	1.51
Newfoundland	62	4	34	.80
Prince Edward Island	—	—	—	—
Nova Scotia	46.5	12.5	41	1.01
New Brunswick	49	12.5	38.5	.89
Quebec	70	6	24	1.50
Ontario	66	5.5	28.5	1.78
Manitoba	66	5	29	1.31
Saskatchewan	63	7	30	1.13
Alberta	62	5	33	1.53
British Columbia	51	5	44	1.62

TABLE II—4

The Percentage Contribution of Beer, Wine, and Spirits to the Apparent
Total Consumption of Absolute Alcohol, and Total Alcohol Consumption
per Capita in Canada and Various European and Other Countries*

(For sources and notes, see page 33.)

		Beer	Wine	Spirits	Imperial gallons per capita of 15 years and older
France	1950	8	73	19	2.80
Italy	1954	2	93	5	2.75
New Zealand	1954	77	5	18	1.91
Germany (West)	1955	44	37	19	1.90
Australia	1952–3	75.5	17.5	7	1.89
Belgium	1952	88	0	12	1.66
U.S.A.	1956	49	11	40	1.64
Switzerland	1945–9	28	51	21	1.60
Canada	1956	64.5	5.5	30	1.51
Peru	1954	13.5	3	83.5	1.32
United Kingdom	1955	82	4	14	1.25
Sweden	1955	24	9	67	1.19
Denmark	1955	77	11	12	1.14
Ireland	1954	73	4	23	0.95
Finland	1955	13	14	73	0.75
Norway	1955	44	8	48	0.66
Iceland	1952	15	5	80	0.59
Netherlands	1953	32	6	62	0.55

*Latest available year in each.

TABLE II–5

TOTAL SALES OF ALCOHOLIC BEVERAGES IN THOUSANDS OF DOLLARS, AND DOLLAR SALES PER CAPITA OF 15 YEARS AND OLDER IN EACH PROVINCE FOR ALL AVAILABLE YEARS

(For sources and notes, see page 33.)

	Newfoundland		Prince Edward I.		Nova Scotia		New Brunswick		Quebec	
	Total sales	Sales per capita	Total sales	Sales per capita	Total sales	Sales per capita	Total sales	Sales per capita	Total sales	Sales per capita
1928	—	—	—	—	—	—	$3,562.4	$13.8	—	—
1929	—	—	—	—	—	—	4,511.4	17.3	—	—
1930	—	—	—	—	—	—	4,809.7	18.4	—	—
1931	—	—	—	—	$4,958.2	$14.3	3,783.8	14.4	—	—
1932	—	—	—	—	3,767.1	10.7	2,794.2	10.4	—	—
1933	—	—	—	—	2,808.7	7.8	2,176.6	8.0	—	—
1934	—	—	—	—	2,818.6	8.0	2,296.1	8.3	—	—
1935	—	—	—	—	3,806.8*	—	2,376.0	8.4	—	—
1936	—	—	—	—	3,831.7	10.1	2,695.9	9.3	—	—
1937	—	—	—	—	4,648.4	12.0	3,535.1	12.0	—	—
1938	—	—	—	—	4,684.9	12.0	3,525.2	11.8	—	—
1939	—	—	—	—	5,483.4	13.8	3,714.8	12.3	—	—
1940	—	—	—	—	8,458.2	20.9	5,209.1	16.9	$35,530.0	$16.0
1941	—	—	—	—	11,449.3	28.0	6,627.0	21.2	39,003.5**	—
1942	—	—	—	—	15,136.8	36.1	8,070.6	25.5	49,765.8	21.5
1943	—	—	—	—	15,324.1	35.6	8,429.0	26.7	65,290.1	27.6
1944	—	—	—	—	17,799.4	41.2	9,464.0	30.0	66,283.2	27.6
1945	—	—	—	—	19,133.0	43.9	10,921.0	34.3	76,942.7	31.6
1946	—	—	—	—	23,316.2	54.6	16,628.8	51.3	90,563.4	36.5
1947	—	—	—	—	21,950.6	51.0	17,199.4	52.6	105,662.1	41.9
1948	—	—	—	—	21,460.6	50.0	16,661.3	50.3	109,048.5	42.6
1949	—	—	—	—	22,274.3	51.6	15,728.9	47.0	114,442.2	43.9
1950	$4,452.2	$20.0	—	—	21,155.4	48.6	13,798.0	41.3	120,475.1	45.4
1951	4,912.9	22.3	—	—	28,341.5†	—	5,962.4‡	—	130,889.3	48.7
1952	5,583.4	24.6	—	—	23,347.1	53.3	16,300.8	48.4	140,849.5	51.0
1953	6,788.5	29.4	$2,736.1	$39.1	26,002.3	58.7	17,856.9	52.4	155,045.7	55.0
1954	11,544.5	48.3	2,970.8	43.1	26,851.8	60.0	17,727.1	51.1	156,496.9	54.2
1955	12,218.0	49.7	3,002.9	42.3	26,782.8	59.9	17,735.1	50.2	156,617.6	53.2
1956	13,202.9	52.6	3,031.0	43.9	27,935.2	60.7	19,709.4	54.6	171,520.6	57.1

*Fourteen-month period.
†Sixteen-month period.
‡Five-month period.
**Eleven-month period.

TABLE II—5 (continued)

Year	Ontario Total sales	Ontario Sales per capita	Manitoba Total sales	Manitoba Sales per capita	Saskatchewan Total sales	Saskatchewan Sales per capita	Alberta Total sales	Alberta Sales per capita	British Columbia Total sales	British Columbia Sales per capita
1923	—	—	—	—	—	—	—	—	$9,276.0	$23.1
1924	—	—	$3,639.2	$9.1	—	—	—	—	11,663.8	28.0
1925	—	—	2,962.9*	—	—	—	—	—	11,409.1	26.4
1926	—	—	3,745.4	9.1	$7,812.7	$15.5	—	—	13,434.3	30.1
1927	—	—	3,793.8	8.9	10,305.2	19.7	—	—	13,805.1	29.9
1928	—	—	3,985.0	9.0	11,708.5	21.6	—	—	13,956.9	29.3
1929	—	—	7,372.6	16.2	14,067.8	25.1	—	—	15,132.9	30.8
1930	—	—	7,620.3	16.2	12,380.7	21.4	—	—	16,498.7	32.5
1931	—	—	6,506.6	13.5	9,158.4	15.4	—	—	14,735.4	28.2
1932	—	—	5,399.0	11.1	5,774.1	9.6	—	—	11,753.9	21.9
1933	$31,052.4	$12.2	4,115.5	8.3	4,787.2	7.9	—	—	8,607.3	15.7
1934	37,028.0	14.3	3,767.4	7.6	4,823.5	7.9	—	—	9,262.1	16.6
1935	36,749.8	14.0	4,208.7	8.4	5,203.9	8.4	—	—	10,195.9	17.9
1936	41,947.7	15.7	4,539.7	8.9	5,735.4	9.1	—	—	11,169.4	19.1
1937	46,109.9	17.0	5,191.4	10.0	6,718.2	10.7	$7,660.7	$14.0	12,746.8	21.4
1938	51,005.7	18.5	5,889.7	11.2	6,042.2	9.6	8,194.3	14.8	14,110.2	23.1
1939	49,638.0	17.8	5,947.6	11.2	6,012.1	9.6	8,645.6	15.5	13,738.1	22.0
1940	53,535.3	18.9	6,653.3	12.4	7,273.9	11.6	9,365.6	16.6	14,960.2	23.6
1941	64,083.6	22.4	7,886.9	14.6	8,509.2	13.5	10,753.4	18.9	17,590.3	27.4
1942	81,487.6	27.7	9,983.3	18.6	10,094.5	16.9	13,197.6	23.8	20,970.0	30.8
1943	93,161.0	31.5	12,367.8	23.0	12,092.1	20.3	16,968.8	30.1	28,711.3	41.0
1944	95,819.5	32.0	12,571.9	23.3	12,155.2	20.4	17,250.5	29.7	24,825.2	34.4
1945	102,885.8	34.0	15,298.5	28.4	13,623.7	22.9	20,564.1	35.5	29,358.4	40.1
1946	135,776.1	44.0	20,267.5	37.9	20,602.4	34.8	27,352.0	47.7	38,734.5	50.2
1947	155,569.0	49.6	21,291.2†	—	25,183.4	42.5	31,736.0	54.3	47,961.5	60.3
1948	170,587.6	53.6	23,743.0	43.6	25,421.9	42.9	33,361.5	55.5	55,249.4	67.3
1949	187,811.1	58.0	25,429.2	46.4	27,657.2	47.4	37,186.7	60.0	56,954.9	68.0
1950	196,790.2	59.7	27,090.2	49.1	29,297.9	50.4	39,850.7	62.6	57,285.5	67.5
1951	210,473.8	62.7	28,007.4	50.6	28,550.7	49.6	41,272.0	63.2	60,575.7	70.1
1952	228,008.2	66.0	30,257.5	53.6	32,165.0	55.2	45,456.6	67.9	66,231.4	75.5
1953	275,227.4	78.2	35,672.2	62.7	37,294.3	62.8	51,664.2	75.4	70,829.5	79.5
1954	288,404.5	80.2	36,827.9	63.6	39,118.5	65.2	53,985.0	76.8	71,946.3	79.1
1955	258,646.3	70.7	33,050.2	56.1	35,646.5	58.9	53,712.7	73.8	73,047.5	78.6
1956	278,684.6	75.1	37,412.8	63.0	34,973.2	57.3	54,770.1	75.6	79,397.3	83.3

*Eleven-month period

†Eleven-month period

TABLE II—6

APPARENT CONSUMPTION OF ABSOLUTE ALCOHOL, SALES OF ALCOHOLIC BEVERAGES, DISPOSABLE INCOME PER CAPITA, AND THE CONSUMER PRICE INDEX IN CANADA, 1926–1956

(For sources and notes, see page 33.)

	Consumption per capita of 15 years and older (Imperial gals.)	Sales per capita of 15 years and older ($)	Disposable income per capita of 15 years and older ($)	Consumer price index (1949 = 100)
1926	0.62	18.4	629	75.9
1927	0.62	19.8	647	74.6
1928	0.77	19.3	678	75.0
1929	0.85	23.2	669	75.8
1930	0.87	22.7	615	75.3
1931	0.76	17.7	501	67.9
1932	0.65	13.1	409	61.7
1933	0.46	11.1	371	58.8
1934	0.46	12.3	412	59.6
1935	0.56	12.6	432	59.9
1936	0.63	13.8	449	61.1
1937	0.67	15.3	498	63.0
1938	0.74	16.2	498	63.7
1939	0.70	16.0	518	63.2
1940	0.74	17.4	583	65.7
1941	0.82	20.2	670	69.6
1942	0.91	25.0	819	72.9
1943	0.98	29.8	861	74.2
1944	0.82	29.9	929	74.6
1945	0.94	33.3	953	75.0
1946	1.20	42.5	1,008	77.5
1947	1.33	47.8	1,065	84.8
1948	1.46	50.3	1 214	97.0
1949	1.41	52.9	1,248	100.0
1950	1.44	53.4	1,318	102.9
1951	1.47	55.7	1,519	113.7
1952	1.46	59.3	1,610	116.5
1953	1.44	66.8	1,664	115.5
1954	1.46	68.0	1,637	116.2
1955	1.39	63.4	1,736	116.4
1956	1.51	67.1	1,885	118.1

TABLE II—7

APPARENT CONSUMPTION OF ABSOLUTE ALCOHOL, SALES OF ALCOHOLIC BEVERAGES,
AND DISPOSABLE INCOME PER CAPITA IN CANADA AND PROVINCES, 1956

(For sources and notes, see page 34.)

	Consumption per capita of 15 years and older (Imperial gals.)	Sales per capita of 15 years and older ($)	Disposable income per capita of 15 years and older ($)
Canada	1.51	67.1	1,885
Newfoundland	.80	52.6	1,151
Prince Edward Island	—	43.9	1,043
Nova Scotia	1.01	60.7	1,426
New Brunswick	.89	54.6	1,327
Quebec	1.50	57.1	1,668
Ontario	1.78	75.1	2,134
Manitoba	1.31	63.0	1,744
Saskatchewan	1.13	57.3	1,879
Alberta	1.53	75.6	2,052
British Columbia	1.62	83.3	2,175

SOURCES AND NOTES

Table II—1, A-J

Figures for the period 1871 to 1893 were based on data in the *Report of the Royal Commission on the Liquor Traffic in Canada*, Ottawa (Queen's Printer, 1895). All other figures were based on data in the *Annual Reports on the Control and Sale of Alcoholic Beverages in Canada* (Ottawa: Dominion Bureau of Statistics). The sales data in these reports were expressed in imperial gallons of beverage. To convert the latter to gallons of absolute alcohol the following values (based on data kindly provided by Mr. A. P. W. Clarke, Chief Chemist, Liquor Control Board of Ontario, personal communication, May 9, 1957) were employed:

> Beer   1871–1956: 5% alcohol by volume
> Wine   1871–1956: 16% alcohol by volume
> Spirits 1871–1942: 43% alcohol by volume
> Spirits 1943–1956: 40% alcohol by volume

It should be noted that the figures shown for wine in the years 1871 to 1893 do not include native wines.

There was considerable variation both among the provinces, and from one period to another in the same province, in the reporting year to which the data tabulated were applicable. Information concerning such differences was not available for the period 1871–1893, but is provided below for all later years. The periods shown apply to both the gallonage data included in this Table, and total sales in dollars provided in Table II—5.

Newfoundland
   1950–1956: year ending March 31.

Prince Edward Island
   1953–1956: year ending March 31.

Nova Scotia
   1931–1934: year ending September 30.
   1935: fourteen months ending November 30.
   1936–1950: year ending November 30.
   1951: sixteen months ending March 31.
   1952–1956: year ending March 31.

New Brunswick
   1928–1950: year ending October 31.
   1951: five months ending March 31.
   1952–1956: year ending March 31.

Quebec
   1928–1940: year ending April 30.
   1941: eleven months ending March 31.
   1942–1956: year ending March 31.

Ontario
   1928–1934: year ending October 31.
   1935: twelve months ending March 31.
   1936–1956: year ending March 31.

31

Manitoba
    1924: year ending August 31.
    1925: eight months ending April 30.
    1926–1946: year ending April 30.
    1947: eleven months ending March 31.
    1948–1956: year ending March 31.

Saskatchewan
    1926–1956: year ending March 31.

Alberta
    1928–1956: year ending March 31.

British Columbia
    1923–1956: year ending March 31.

Per capita figures were calculated on the basis of population data provided in Table V—1, B-K. The age group 15 years and older was employed as the best available estimate for general use of the size of the drinking population (see notes to Table I—3). Thus, the proportion of actual users of alcoholic beverages in the population is only available for a limited number of years, and is not available for all provinces individually (see Part I). It is safe to assume that rates calculated in this manner, unless offset by other factors, represent conservative estimates of per capita consumption by users of alcoholic beverages. However, it should be kept in mind that increases or decreases in such rates may reflect changes in the number of users in the population, rather than in the average amount consumed by users.

See also notes to Table II—2.

Table II—2
Figures for the years 1871–1893, and 1953–1956, inclusive, were based on the total of available provincial data in each of these years, as given in Table II—1, A-J. Figures for the period 1922–1952 were based on the special estimates of apparent national consumption provided in the *Annual Reports on the Control and Sale of Alcoholic Beverages in Canada* (Ottawa: Dominion Bureau of Statistics, 1950–1952). These estimates were calculated on the basis of quantities produced and other data, and are more comprehensive than estimates based on provincial gallonage data, since the latter are more or less incompletely reported in nearly all available years. Fortunately, all but one province (P.E.I.) reported gallonage data for 1955 and 1956, and all but two (P.E.I. and N.B.) for 1953 and 1954. All provinces reported such data for the period 1874–1893, all but one (P.E.I.) for the years 1872 and 1873, and all but two (P.E.I. and B.C.) for the year 1871. Accordingly, it seemed justifiable to extend the Dominion Bureau series to include estimates based on provincial data in these years.

The Yukon and Northwest Territories were included in the national estimates reported by the Dominion Bureau for the period 1922–1952. These areas were not included in the gallonage data for any other years, or in the population figures employed to calculate per capita estimates (see Table V—1, A-K). However, available information indicates that their combined contribution to national sales of alcoholic beverages has probably at no time exceeded one per cent.

Cognizance should be taken of the fact that the estimates of consumption reported for the period 1922–1952, "take no account of increases or decreases in the quantities held in stock by the [provincial] Boards . . . [which] may, in certain years, buy

32

heavily to replenish stock or create reserves; such purchases would unduly weight the consumption figures for these years." It is also important to note that all of the data "refer to the consumption of alcoholic beverages in Canada— not to consumption by Canadians. Temporary additions to Canada's population through tourist travel are, at certain seasons, extremely large. . . . Sales of alcoholic beverages to certain of these visitors undoubtedly reach considerable proportions. Precise measurement is impossible, however, since no separate record is kept by the [provincial] Liquor boards of sales to non-residents of Canada" (*The Control and Sale of Alcoholic Beverages*, 1952, p. 21).

Finally, when concern is with the evaluation of time trends in per capita consumption, it is well to have in mind the following historical information regarding prohibition in Canada: "During the years 1916 and 1917, as a war policy, legislation prohibiting the sale of alcoholic liquors, except for medicinal and scientific purposes, was passed in all the provinces except Quebec where similar legislation was passed in 1919. The prohibition extended to the sale of beer and wine except in Quebec. Native wine could be sold, however, in Ontario. In aid of provincial legislation prohibiting or restricting the sale of intoxicating liquors, the Dominion Government in 1916 passed a law making it an offence to send intoxicating liquor into any province to be dealt in contrary to the law of that province. . . . After the war the provinces continued under prohibition for varying periods. . . . During 1921 Quebec and British Columbia discarded the existing prohibition laws and adopted the policy of liquor sale under government control. The same course was followed by Manitoba in 1923, Alberta in 1924, Saskatchewan in 1925, Ontario and New Brunswick in 1927 and Nova Scotia in 1930" (*The Control and Sale of Alcoholic Beverages*, 1936, p. 4). Parenthetically, Prince Edward Island retained its prohibition laws until 1948.

See also notes to Table II—1, A–J.

Table II—3
Figures for Canada were taken from Table II—2; those shown for each province were based on the data provided in Table II—1, A-J.

Table II—4
The figures for Canada were taken from Table II—2; all other figures were based on data in M. Keller & V. Efron, *Selected Statistical Tables on Alcoholic Beverages (1850–1956) and on Alcoholism (1910–1955)* (New Haven: *Journal of Studies on Alcohol, Inc., 1957*), Table 7.

Table II—5
Total sales of alcoholic beverages in dollars were obtained from the *Annual Reports on the Control and Sale of Alcoholic Beverages in Canada*. Per capita sales were calculated on the basis of population data provided in Table V—1, B-K. For variations in the reporting year to which the data were applicable, and other pertinent information, see notes to Table II—1, A-J.

Table II—6
Estimates of per capita consumption were taken from Table II—2; per capita sales in dollars were based on the total of available provincial data in each year (see Table II—5), and appropriately corrected population figures (see Table V—1, A-K). Estimates of per capita income were calculated on the basis of data provided in *National Accounts: Income and Expenditure, 1926–1956* (Ottawa: Dominion

Bureau of Statistics), Table 30. These estimates refer to personal disposable, i.e., total personal income less personal direct taxes. Consumer price indexes (formerly cost-of-living index) for the years 1926–1952, inclusive, were obtained from Prices & Price Indexes 1949–1952, op. cit.; indexes for the years 1953–6, inclusive, were provided through the kindness of Mr. Frank Curry, Unit Head, Consumer Prices, Prices Section, Dominion Bureau of Statistics, Ottawa (personal communication, June 11, 1958).

Population figures for the age group of 15 years and older (Table V—1, A) were employed to calculate estimates of per capita income since this age group has been utilized throughout as the best available estimate, of the size of the drinking population (see notes to Tables I—3 and II—1, A-J).

See also notes to Table II—2.

Table II—7

For the sources of the figures shown for Canada, see notes to Table II—6. Estimates of per capita consumption, and per capita sales in dollars for the provinces were taken from Table II—1, A-J and Table II—5, respectively. Personal income data by province were obtained from the same source as employed in the case of the Dominion, and per capita estimates were calculated on the same basis (see notes to Table II—6).

It should be noted that the personal income data employed in the case of British Columbia included the Yukon and Northwest Territories, which were not included in the population figures employed to calculate per capita esimates. However, personal income in these areas amounted to less than 3 per cent of that reported for British Columbia during the period 1951–1956.

See also notes to Table II—1, A-J.

PART III

Convictions for Offences involving Alcohol

TABLE III—1

CONVICTIONS FOR DRUNKENNESS, FOR OFFENCES UNDER THE LIQUOR CONTROL
ACTS, AND FOR ALL TYPES OF OFFENCE IN CANADA AND PROVINCES, 1881–1955

(For sources and notes, see page 77.)

	Convictions for drunkenness			Convictions under Liquor Control Acts	Convictions for all offences
	Male	Female	Total		
		A. Canada			
1881	—	—	9,575	1,739	29,021
1882	—	—	11,509	1,672	31,297
1883	—	—	12,776	2,006	33,343
1884	—	—	9,815	1,820	29,497
1885	—	—	11,215	2,052	33,746
1886	—	—	11,081	2,622	33,814
1887	—	—	11,647	3,733	34,416
1888	—	—	12,740	4,227	37,498
1889	—	—	13,748	2,990	38,119
1890	—	—	13,964	2,164	38,229
1891	—	—	12,915	2,265	37,062
1892	—	—	11,306	2,006	34,585
1893	—	—	11,519	2,618	34,897
1894	10,189	1,175	11,364	2,095	35,289
1895	10,315	1,023	11,338	2,109	36,557
1896	9,929	1,141	11,070	1,931	36,243
1897	9,242	1,050	10,292	2,027	36,401
1898	9,627	1,050	10,677	2,071	36,132
1899	9,303	1,025	10,328	1,933	35,882
1900	10,302	1,150	11,452	1,819	38,357
1901	10,680	1,186	11,866	2,006	39,419
1902	11,446	1,121	12,567	2,242	41,202
1903	14,127	1,127	15,254	2,722	46,382
1904	16,178	1,374	17,552	2,671	50,292
1905	18,535	1,556	20,091	2,905	57,130
1906	21,499	1,246	22,745	2,910	63,299
1907	28,316	1,378	29,694	3,457	78,814
1908	29,598	1,374	30,972	3,540	88,352
1909	29,548	1,438	30,986	3,958	89,648
1910	32,634	1,318	33,952	4,621	102,648
1911	39,809	1,500	41,309	4,726	113,057
1912	51,516	1,569	53,085	5,605	146,247
1913	59,025	1,890	60,915	5,928	172,954
1914	57,940	2,066	60,006	5,822	182,811
1915	39,310	1,791	41,101	5,425	152,885
1916	31,065	1,612	32,677	6,237	123,615
1917	26,515	1,342	27,857	7,324	113,905
1918	20,031	976	21,007	7,449	123,194
1919	23,136	1,072	24,208	7,377	129,982

TABLE III—1 (*continued*)

	Convictions for drunkenness			Convictions under Liquor Control Acts	Convictions for all offences
	Male	Female	Total		
A. Canada (*continued*)					
1920	38,540	1,219	39,759	10,239	162,653
1921	33,470	890	34,360	10,458	177,060
1922	24,207	829	25,036	8,507	151,980
1923	24,694	850	25,544	10,074	152,638
1924	26,301	1,026	27,327	10,445	159,218
1925	25,659	1,077	26,736	11,618	168,949
1926	27,281	1,020	28,301	13,510	187,265
1927	29,982	1,163	31,145	12,464	211,981
1928	32,059	1,131	33,190	15,209	267,349
1929	37,643	1,141	38,784	19,311	314,000
1930	34,625	1,129	35,754	18,111	337,082
1931	28,127	980	29,107	16,162	359,156
1932	21,769	876	22,645	12,204	329,195
1933	18,053	828	18,881	10,472	325,510
1934	19,784	964	20,748	10,742	360,359
1935	24,365	1,244	25,609	8,808	396,077
1936	26,838	1,571	28,409	10,040	413,664
1937	32,528	2,045	34,573	11,107	457,223
1938	34,882	1,985	36,867	12,419	458,133
1939	34,164	1,807	35,971	13,462	476,494
1940	35,653	2,127	37,780	12,875	502,612
1941	37,594	2,341	39,935	15,316	589,953
1942	41,901	2,838	44,739	16,840	620,465
1943	39,201	3,025	42,226	15,016	506,775
1944	38,453	3,001	41,454	16,951	472,746
1945	43,211	3,439	46,650	22,185	497,446
1946	59,707	4,246	63,953	33,159	706,005
1947	66,067	4,580	70,647	28,287	795,705
1948	65,688	4,729	70,417	27,632	917,525
1949	70,802	4,994	75,796	28,249	1,021,742
1950	70,554	5,078	75,632	31,640	1,225,724
1951	77,966	5,615	83,581	28,273	1,347,417
1952	79,623	5,421	85,044	32,998	1,605,352
1953	84,643	5,907	90,550	34,619	1,806,571
1954	87,610	6,482	94,092	36,452	2,023,653
1955	86,346	6,799	93,145	36,389	2,193,967
B. Newfoundland					
1951	791	53	844	371	5,575
1952	747	39	786	475	6,819
1953	968	77	1,045	441	6,899
1954	853	13	866	411	7,865
1955	968	47	1,015	571	9,373

TABLE III—1 (*continued*)

	Convictions for drunkenness			Convictions under Liquor Control Acts	Convictions for all offences
	Male	Female	Total		
C. Prince Edward Island					
1881	—	—	261	50	527
1882	—	—	247	77	514
1883	—	—	244	53	530
1884	—	—	246	77	527
1885	—	—	328	90	698
1886	—	—	359	72	658
1887	—	—	274	80	510
1888	—	—	287	91	469
1889	—	—	330	69	535
1890	—	—	287	75	477
1891	—	—	311	90	555
1892	—	—	301	75	576
1893	—	—	233	37	359
1894	170	4	174	84	461
1895	162	0	162	82	374
1896	125	4	129	70	305
1897	287	5	292	114	561
1898	285	3	288	31	460
1899	318	2	320	19	452
1900	319	8	327	9	429
1901	239	2	241	17	338
1902	228	2	230	38	360
1903	272	2	274	50	438
1904	285	3	288	59	449
1905	171	1	172	74	368
1906	118	2	120	37	237
1907	144	0	144	23	234
1908	184	0	184	43	293
1909	157	3	160	38	302
1910	182	1	183	40	384
1911	235	3	238	38	396
1912	308	1	309	36	448
1913	323	1	324	26	455
1914	342	0	342	72	523
1915	230	1	231	42	362
1916	219	0	219	75	419
1917	206	1	207	36	356
1918	96	0	96	42	246
1919	115	1	116	37	267
1920	120	0	120	23	359
1921	141	3	144	44	397
1922	159	3	162	28	336
1923	164	0	164	39	334

TABLE III—1 (*continued*)

	Convictions for drunkenness			Convictions under Liquor Control Acts	Convictions for all offences
	Male	Female	Total		
C. Prince Edward Island (*continued*)					
1924	94	0	94	29	257
1925	112	0	112	51	238
1926	168	0	168	53	359
1927	182	0	182	66	406
1928	263	0	263	69	705
1929	404	2	406	81	838
1930	390	3	393	98	965
1931	445	1	446	52	895
1932	353	2	355	50	903
1933	297	0	297	52	725
1934	400	1	401	80	821
1935	472	3	475	79	983
1936	552	6	558	37	1,031
1937	542	17	559	166	1,536
1938	575	20	595	333	1,722
1939	523	23	546	230	1,561
1940	454	13	467	215	1,488
1941	524	15	539	250	1,871
1942	583	23	606	188	1,726
1943	514	18	332	118	1,207
1944	383	12	395	56	1,549
1945	590	22	612	155	1,625
1946	1,423	55	1,478	374	3,035
1947	1,171	16	1,187	354	2,983
1948	958	11	969	329	2,823
1949	1,072	17	1,089	439	3,248
1950	892	15	907	268	2,220
1951	755	4	759	266	2,306
1952	1,024	25	1,049	284	2,672
1953	993	14	1,007	280	2,820
1954	962	4	966	368	3,133
1955	1,032	1	1,033	464	3,676
D. Nova Scotia					
1881	—	—	737	46	1,590
1882	—	—	563	20	1,294
1883	—	—	600	58	1,448
1884	—	—	591	51	1,491
1885	—	—	768	63	1,701
1886	—	—	667	60	1,542
1887	—	—	462	71	1,266
1888	—	—	501	83	1,203
1889	—	—	657	89	1,373

TABLE III—1 (*continued*)

	Convictions for drunkenness			Convictions under Liquor Control Acts	Convictions for all offences
	Male	Female	Total		
		D. Nova Scotia (*continued*)			
1890	—	—	642	130	1,479
1891	—	—	635	118	1,478
1892	—	—	676	121	1,619
1893	—	—	938	154	1,954
1894	1,149	109	1,258	166	2,448
1895	1,461	106	1,567	185	3,177
1896	1,508	143	1,651	193	3,321
1897	1,109	90	1,199	209	2,676
1898	1,133	135	1,268	212	2,680
1899	917	105	1,022	169	2,259
1900	1,176	79	1,255	153	2,595
1901	1,297	90	1,387	167	2,977
1902	1,926	86	2,012	207	3,877
1903	2,649	77	2,726	422	4,906
1904	2,257	87	2,344	371	4,253
1905	2,423	106	2,529	446	4,618
1906	2,812	107	2,919	540	5,057
1907	2,858	117	2,975	490	5,109
1908	2,709	91	2,800	384	5,135
1909	2,610	79	2,689	410	4,880
1910	3,034	97	3,131	494	6,097
1911	3,080	69	3,149	592	5,689
1912	3,608	85	3,693	551	6,649
1913	3,888	67	3,955	502	7,038
1914	3,907	92	3,999	660	7,379
1915	3,367	69	3,436	633	6,724
1916	3,512	102	3,614	646	6,568
1917	2,464	82	2,546	449	5,282
1918	2,369	66	2,435	412	5,511
1919	2,807	72	2,879	479	6,300
1920	3,046	94	3,140	394	6,503
1921	2,110	46	2,156	362	5,572
1922	1,450	42	1,492	267	4,033
1923	1,361	31	1,392	264	3,433
1924	1,430	26	1,456	293	3,950
1925	1,430	36	1,466	235	3,414
1926	1,862	36	1,898	499	4,320
1927	2,014	39	2,053	610	5,042
1928	2,140	36	2,176	688	5,390
1929	3,224	60	3,284	804	7,100
1930	3,172	64	3,236	532	7,174
1931	2,095	42	2,137	588	6,508
1932	1,369	33	1,402	353	4,645

TABLE III—1 (*continued*)

	Convictions for drunkenness			Convictions under Liquor Control Acts	Convictions for all offences
	Male	Female	Total		
D. Nova Scotia (*continued*)					
1933	1,437	41	1,478	586	5,082
1934	1,452	34	1,486	750	5,208
1935	1,893	40	1,933	699	5,820
1936	2,140	81	2,221	698	6,740
1937	2,479	98	2,577	706	7,330
1938	2,539	89	2,628	794	7,821
1939	2,375	88	2,463	1,181	9,138
1940	3,499	108	3,607	1,149	10,711
1941	3,550	104	3,654	1,273	11,929
1942	4,225	162	4,387	1,323	12,032
1943	2,294	86	2,380	1,369	10,582
1944	1,962	106	2,068	2,240	10,542
1945	2,899	165	3,064	2,324	11,902
1946	4,574	180	4,754	3,436	15,176
1947	4,764	143	4,907	2,503	13,862
1948	4,002	149	4,151	2,274	15,249
1949	4,204	159	4,363	2,053	14,207
1950	3,789	142	3,931	2,192	14,694
1951	4,306	126	4,432	2,273	16,209
1952	5,071	386	5,457	2,236	16,300
1953	6,122	256	6,378	2,124	18,991
1954	5,941	197	5,941	2,285	19,840
1955	6,382	145	6,527	2,056	21,261
E. New Brunswick					
1881	—	—	1,130	90	1,859
1882	—	—	1,353	83	2,278
1883	—	—	1,528	129	2,571
1884	—	—	1,402	183.	2,453
1885	—	—	1,300	54	2,047
1886	—	—	1,290	153	2,176
1887	—	—	1,011	228	1,860
1888	—	—	1,141	222	2,072
1889	—	—	1,383	159	2,246
1890	—	—	1,561	326	2,597
1891	—	—	1,628	245	2,540
1892	—	—	1,291	268	2,267
1893	—	—	1,365	444	2,423
1894	1,134	93	1,227	337	2,205
1895	1,102	103	1,205	364	2,230
1896	1,140	98	1,238	435	2,297
1897	1,126	102	1,228	340	2,274
1898	1,197	93	1,290	362	2,354

TABLE III—1 (*continued*)

	Convictions for drunkenness			Convictions under Liquor Control Acts	Convictions for all offences
	Male	Female	Total		
E. New Brunswick (*continued*)					
1899	1,197	73	1,270	324	2,261
1900	1,213	75	1,288	301	2,311
1901	1,228	71	1,299	329	2,292
1902	1,331	72	1,403	302	2,378
1903	1,389	69	1,458	294	2,433
1904	1,628	48	1,676	375	2,746
1905	1,679	55	1,734	327	2,606
1906	1,793	50	1,843	309	2,700
1907	1,963	55	2,018	395	2,984
1908	1,829	52	1,881	372	2,947
1909	1,665	29	1,694	353	2,637
1910	1,529	33	1,562	367	2,595
1911	1,918	26	1,944	278	2,912
1912	2,075	41	2,116	361	3,157
1913	2,041	32	2,073	447	3,324
1914	1,734	31	1,765	365	3,101
1915	1,668	26	1,694	390	3,111
1916	1,661	35	1,696	352	2,960
1917	1,492	24	1,516	312	2,896
1918	693	11	704	288	1,945
1919	1,330	20	1,350	387	2,780
1920	1,854	28	1,882	585	3,839
1921	1,237	27	1,264	419	3,070
1922	1,071	17	1,088	366	2,603
1923	1,061	13	1,074	364	2,327
1924	1,156	20	1,176	375	2,723
1925	1,163	8	1,171	319	2,661
1926	1,218	16	1,234	393	2,640
1927	1,375	22	1,397	271	2,852
1928	1,246	39	1,285	478	3,396
1929	1,766	48	1,814	486	4,390
1930	1,668	38	1,706	469	4,426
1931	1,507	34	1,541	541	4,994
1932	1,099	43	1,142	489	4,355
1933	1,079	48	1,127	559	3,962
1934	1,465	40	1,505	622	4,123
1935	1,698	57	1,755	567	4,544
1936	2,063	124	2,187	610	5,435
1937	2,662	147	2,809	596	6,465
1938	2,607	123	2,730	487	6,211
1939	2,076	103	2,179	619	6,202
1940	2,410	105	2,515	379	7,344
1941	3,188	144	3,332	431	8,888

TABLE III—1 (*continued*)

	Convictions for drunkenness			Convictions under Liquor Control Acts	Convictions for all offences
	Male	Female	Total		
E. New Brunswick (*continued*)					
1942	4,080	137	4,217	477	9,233
1943	3,357	132	3,489	473	8,830
1944	4,143	149	4,292	814	10,843
1945	3,984	174	4,158	911	11,066
1946	7,513	241	7,754	1,411	15,417
1947	6,408	176	6,584	1,742	15,565
1948	4,770	130	4,900	1,274	13,359
1949	4,973	152	5,125	1,278	14,030
1950	4,817	163	4,980	1,172	22,788
1951	5,900	136	6,036	818	26,536
1952	6,357	193	6,550	1,172	32,807
1953	6,560	152	6,712	1,221	34,128
1954	6,764	193	6,975	979	35,968
1955	5,980	87	6,067	1,014	39,497
F. Quebec					
1881	—	—	1,450	391	6,430
1882	—	—	1,972	506	6,698
1883	—	—	1,546	637	6,662
1884	—	—	1,624	320	6,190
1885	—	—	2,163	439	7,223
1886	—	—	2,367	492	7,854
1887	—	—	2,947	600	8,527
1888	—	—	3,360	628	9,190
1889	—	—	3,412	572	9,521
1890	—	—	3,999	372	10,301
1891	—	—	4,199	434	10,743
1892	—	—	3,832	304	10,493
1893	—	—	3,778	387	9,762
1894	3,896	372	4,272	277	10,847
1895	3,956	351	4,307	287	11,349
1896	3,879	396	4,275	384	10,737
1897	3,450	419	3,869	405	10,608
1898	3,383	390	3,773	493	10,026
1899	3,088	393	3,481	529	10,275
1900	2,802	407	3,209	458	9,917
1901	2,573	400	2,973	457	9,384
1902	2,441	342	2,783	600	9,346
1903	2,582	349	2,931	660	9,944
1904	3,404	582	3,986	583	11,400
1905	4,055	726	4,781	856	13,798
1906	4,308	494	4,802	858	14,524

TABLE III—1 (continued)

	Convictions for drunkenness			Convictions under Liquor Control Acts	Convictions for all offences
	Male	Female	Total		
	F. Quebec (continued)				
1907	5,038	465	5,503	706	15,340
1908	6,395	448	6,843	864	18,565
1909	6,406	550	6,956	710	18,855
1910	5,135	422	5,557	893	18,514
1911	6,283	522	6,805	1,032	19,773
1912	9,140	723	9,863	859	26,850
1913	11,360	905	12,265	791	32,703
1914	11,915	861	12,776	882	34,149
1915	8,151	788	8,939	1,021	27,205
1916	6,434	674	7,108	1,015	24,591
1917	7,396	629	8,025	1,076	25,936
1918	6,228	452	6,680	1,155	29,121
1919	6,221	495	7,116	1,479	34,801
1920	11,421	442	11,863	1,975	44,089
1921	9,607	337	9,944	1,384	49,033
1922	6,833	270	7,103	954	34,326
1923	6,061	199	6,260	1,724	30,218
1924	5,878	268	6,146	1,549	25,532
1925	6,042	300	6,342	1,919	28,448
1926	5,081	283	5,364	2,014	27,481
1927	6,699	301	7,000	2,025	32,353
1928	6,061	301	6,362	2,096	33,601
1929	8,050	278	8,328	3,392	55,879
1930	7,331	318	7,649	3,043	65,638
1931	7,192	269	7,461	2,956	105,118
1932	5,619	294	5,913	2,379	119,218
1933	4,286	289	4,575	1,755	125,146
1934	4,482	294	4,776	2,325	123,000
1935	4,390	315	4,705	1,776	127,853
1936	4,964	368	5,332	1,252	120,751
1937	6,966	578	7,544	1,376	107,185
1938	6,756	464	7,220	1,837	99,720
1939	6,193	234	6,427	2,423	102,411
1940	6,706	280	6,986	2,102	106,117
1941	7,785	507	8,292	3,206	163,844
1942	9,791	609	10,400	3,037	205,941
1943	9,727	636	10,363	2,070	193,094
1944	8,337	506	8,843	1,287	156,979
1945	9,754	582	10,336	2,626	168,172
1946	6,781	386	7,167	2,274	185,574
1947	10,275	731	11,006	1,494	196,114
1948	10,352	663	11,015	1,519	236,678
1949	9,757	662	10,419	1,969	241,364

TABLE III—1 (continued)

	Convictions for drunkenness			Convictions under Liquor Control Acts	Convictions for all offences
	Male	Female	Total		
F. Quebec (continued)					
1950	10,142	800	10,942	3,121	289,775
1951	9,363	859	10,222	1,467	275,690
1952	10,204	498	10,702	777	321,420
1953	8,677	426	9,103	1,304	361,941
1954	10,109	554	10,663	1,203	453,090
1955	9,205	581	9,786	1,322	454,952
G. Ontario					
1881	—	—	5,238	965	17,110
1882	—	—	5,548	833	17,460
1883	—	—	6,086	914	17,678
1884	—	—	4,694	1,000	16,276
1885	—	—	5,868	1,235	20,097
1886	—	—	5,453	1,646	19,174
1887	—	—	6,200	2,664	20,630
1888	—	—	6,633	3,108	23,017
1889	—	—	7,059	1,982	22,527
1890	—	—	6,553	1,131	21,301
1891	—	—	4,973	1,220	19,389
1892	—	—	3,967	1,069	17,081
1893	—	—	3,787	1,347	17,362
1894	2,813	454	3,267	1,062	16,715
1895	2,798	334	3,132	968	16,681
1896	2,310	314	2,624	742	16,892
1897	2,210	255	2,465	782	17,006
1898	2,260	260	2,520	807	16,811
1899	2,464	300	2,764	761	16,784
1900	2,981	389	3,370	749	18,419
1901	3,474	426	3,900	820	19,037
1902	3,523	421	3,944	784	19,462
1903	4,609	434	5,043	1,051	21,996
1904	4,996	469	5,465	1,028	22,817
1905	5,576	471	6,047	861	24,870
1906	7,050	409	7,459	877	27,574
1907	8,460	499	8,959	1,016	30,411
1908	8,892	525	9,417	1,140	34,890
1909	9,480	555	10,035	1,644	36,635
1910	10,237	480	10,717	1,701	41,401
1911	10,849	498	11,347	1,759	40,782
1912	12,314	471	12,785	2,117	48,552
1913	15,754	482	16,236	2,167	58,799

TABLE III—1 (*continued*)

	Convictions for drunkenness			Convictions under Liquor Control Acts	Convictions for all offences
	Male	Female	Total		
G. Ontario (*continued*)					
1914	17,153	550	17,703	2,328	65,806
1915	12,067	486	12,553	2,018	58,876
1916	11,333	395	11,728	2,002	49,620
1917	10,585	360	10,945	2,927	49,579
1918	7,696	236	7,932	3,410	54,761
1919	8,241	257	8,498	3,353	53,215
1920	14,661	360	15,021	4,385	63,463
1921	14,251	247	14,498	4,938	74,127
1922	9,819	244	10,063	3,246	70,036
1923	11,098	272	11,370	3,958	71,525
1924	12,655	338	12,993	4,678	80,948
1925	11,466	345	11,811	5,047	87,221
1926	13,418	334	13,752	6,362	97,309
1927	13,939	395	14,334	5,620	109,307
1928	15,568	363	15,931	7,812	155,638
1929	17,259	361	17,620	9,034	162,874
1930	15,632	338	15,970	8,995	175,687
1931	12,068	336	12,404	8,044	165,451
1932	10,075	313	10,388	6,057	143,802
1933	8,421	303	8,724	5,067	137,741
1934	8,741	319	9,060	4,324	172,656
1935	11,839	547	12,386	3,225	203,416
1936	12,436	613	13,049	4,185	218,338
1937	15,185	775	15,960	4,788	251,878
1938	16,697	888	17,585	5,873	255,472
1939	17,225	895	18,120	5,144	267,413
1940	16,728	1,095	17,823	5,372	284,724
1941	16,662	1,169	17,831	6,346	304,735
1942	16,367	1,255	17,622	6,901	300,310
1943	16,103	1,379	17,482	6,751	221,006
1944	15,847	1,411	17,258	8,332	217,551
1945	18,158	1,415	19,573	10,655	227,000
1946	27,672	2,026	29,698	15,779	375,533
1947	29,257	1,961	31,218	12,889	427,512
1948	31,348	2,098	33,446	13,891	463,616
1949	31,740	2,057	33,797	14,339	528,140
1950	33,037	2,319	35,356	15,761	635,159
1951	36,099	2,478	38,577	14,104	688,292
1952	33,905	2,439	36,344	15,050	836,349
1953	35,414	2,694	38,108	17,137	978,535
1954	35,766	2,695	38,461	18,351	1,084,834
1955	36,488	2,977	39,465	18,256	1,242,772

TABLE III—1 (*continued*)

	Convictions for drunkenness			Convictions under Liquor Control Acts	Convictions for all offences
	Male	Female	Total		
		H. Manitoba			
1881	—	—	534	156	1,054
1882	—	—	1,504	110	2,505
1883	—	—	2,258	67	3,444
1884	—	—	1,085	53	2,147
1885	—	—	711	100	1,683
1886	—	—	631	79	1,411
1887	—	—	529	12	891
1888	—	—	479	1	748
1889	—	—	591	30	1,115
1890	—	—	486	15	993
1891	—	—	518	11	997
1892	—	—	633	21	1,228
1893	—	—	592	60	1,300
1894	506	79	585	16	1,176
1895	388	79	467	39	1,185
1896	487	86	573	38	1,329
1897	505	104	609	52	1,477
1898	484	89	573	36	1,328
1899	564	72	636	30	1,489
1900	697	79	776	34	1,692
1901	743	91	834	60	2,220
1902	940	63	1,003	50	2,272
1903	1,387	79	1,466	76	3,063
1904	2,425	80	2,505	122	5,379
1905	3,408	136	3,544	85	7,398
1906	3,787	118	3,905	51	9,255
1907	4,453	149	4,602	33	9,592
1908	3,514	125	3,639	75	8,626
1909	3,466	124	3,590	41	9,093
1910	4,117	172	4,289	46	10,026
1911	5,624	208	5,832	46	13,413
1912	6,831	94	6,925	85	15,287
1913	7,323	170	7,493	166	18,095
1914	5,974	219	6,193	166	16,334
1915	3,958	196	4,154	124	12,843
1916	2,905	209	3,114	172	9,052
1917	975	110	1,085	289	8,155
1918	1,017	106	1,123	230	8,662
1919	1,469	101	1,570	175	9,514
1920	2,217	113	2.330	380	12,516
1921	1,372	57	1,429	427	11,610
1922	1,521	102	1,623	392	10,718

TABLE III—1 (*continued*)

	Convictions for drunkenness			Convictions under Liquor Control Acts	Convictions for all offences
	Male	Female	Total		
H. Manitoba (*continued*)					
1923	1,588	92	1,680	542	12,471
1924	1,776	172	1,948	452	12,349
1925	1,804	144	1,948	512	11,939
1926	1,737	134	1,871	786	15,296
1927	1,736	147	1,883	627	17,877
1928	1,752	111	1,863	598	21,593
1929	1,761	69	1,830	1,399	28,524
1930	1,322	70	1,392	1,180	29,151
1931	1,007	82	1,089	1,144	25,727
1932	958	65	1,023	900	21,200
1933	688	49	737	708	18,063
1934	754	72	826	826	19,556
1935	962	92	1,054	792	18,067
1936	1,044	81	1,125	940	20,107
1937	973	77	1,050	849	31,339
1938	1,179	107	1,286	886	35,789
1939	866	119	985	1,052	34,687
1940	1,398	129	1,527	997	34,371
1941	1,363	109	1,472	624	35,292
1942	1,369	211	1,580	1,130	34,628
1943	1,679	206	1,885	1,086	24,046
1944	1,281	170	1,451	1,057	25,022
1945	1,837	203	2,040	1,429	25,337
1946	2,460	225	2,685	2,059	38,848
1947	2,269	241	2,510	2,229	49,978
1948	2,462	367	2,829	1,921	55,990
1949	3,148	465	3,613	1,574	74,576
1950	2,657	327	2,984	1,980	81,835
1951	2,756	342	3,098	1,961	120,783
1952	2,901	371	3,272	2,314	137,604
1953	3,356	373	3,729	2,013	138,491
1954	3,428	464	3,892	2,501	144,093
1955	3,156	460	3,616	2,102	113,932
I. Saskatchewan					
1907	1,722	19	1,741	219	5,319
1908	1,297	21	1,318	121	5,199
1909	1,325	9	1,334	164	5,120
1910	1,872	13	1,885	248	7,248
1911	2,323	36	2,359	240	8,294
1912	2,446	16	2,462	366	10,404
1913	2,951	19	2,970	528	13,328

TABLE III—1 (*continued*)

	Convictions for drunkenness			Convictions under Liquor Control Acts	Convictions for all offences
	Male	Female	Total		
I. Saskatchewan (*continued*)					
1914	2,127	15	2,142	404	13,782
1915	1,318	14	1,332	378	11,672
1916	1,047	15	1,062	967	11,016
1917	751	19	770	774	7,072
1918	422	12	434	422	7,635
1919	597	21	618	434	7,315
1920	897	22	919	452	7,991
1921	688	20	708	583	7,384
1922	795	21	816	708	8,267
1923	854	30	884	997	9,792
1924	483	22	505	966	8,921
1925	642	26	668	1,078	9,674
1926	479	8	487	1,231	10,666
1927	610	8	618	1,245	9,735
1928	1,007	7	1,014	1,174	10,869
1929	787	7	794	1,542	13,331
1930	655	19	674	1,392	13,929
1931	454	12	466	1,042	13,407
1932	312	7	319	629	9,431
1933	277	9	286	553	8,404
1934	286	18	304	543	8,076
1935	366	13	379	506	7,725
1936	409	9	418	570	7,944
1937	409	16	425	734	10,663
1938	834	14	848	606	9,668
1939	876	19	895	593	11,597
1940	555	25	580	927	12,162
1941	567	24	591	894	13,605
1942	545	25	570	982	11,162
1943	725	53	778	1,099	10,023
1944	794	70	864	1,010	9,862
1945	937	73	1,010	1,416	11,200
1946	1,737	110	1,847	2,697	16,488
1947	1,711	91	1,802	2,712	17,435
1948	1,339	53	1,392	2,311	17,225
1949	1,413	84	1,497	2,418	18,175
1950	1,387	116	1,503	2,478	24,393
1951	1,787	128	1,915	2,005	24,262
1952	2,117	147	2,264	2,527	33,265
1953	2,546	182	2,728	3,146	36,757
1954	2,489	181	2,670	3,484	48,439
1955	2,888	259	3,147	3,480	48,621

TABLE III—1 (*continued*)

	Convictions for drunkenness			Convictions under Liquor Control Acts	Convictions for all offences
	Male	Female	Total		
J. Alberta					
1907	1,441	18	1,459	193	4,473
1908	1,958	32	1,990	267	6,121
1909	2,178	36	2,214	250	6,878
1910	3,496	47	3,543	396	9,515
1911	4,001	40	4,041	423	10,269
1912	6,620	37	6,657	605	16,775
1913	7,223	60	7,283	560	19,426
1914	5,620	90	5,710	551	19,043
1915	2,752	50	2,802	573	14,419
1916	1,748	61	1,809	713	11,426
1917	372	19	391	885	6,627
1918	796	29	825	678	7,633
1919	1,015	42	1,057	436	7,001
1920	1,486	50	1,536	618	8,459
1921	1,776	62	1,838	907	9,847
1922	1,535	73	1,608	1,043	8,937
1923	1,223	54	1,277	990	9,782
1924	1,427	37	1,464	817	9,765
1925	1,321	53	1,374	758	9,094
1926	1,365	48	1,413	737	9,605
1927	1,138	44	1,182	814	10,284
1928	1,462	76	1,538	944	12,628
1929	1,731	79	1,810	1,017	16,140
1930	1,508	43	1,551	970	15,429
1931	1,140	51	1,191	888	16,000
1932	864	44	908	557	10,421
1933	561	28	589	410	12,242
1934	576	33	609	452	10,604
1935	655	37	692	472	10,822
1936	744	41	785	784	11,948
1937	858	71	929	1,018	14,499
1938	867	55	922	810	14,592
1939	1,053	77	1,130	913	17,903
1940	1,155	116	1,271	831	19,113
1941	1,293	60	1,353	1,298	18,697
1942	1,258	135	1,393	1,294	17,736
1943	1,316	146	1,462	1,106	14,385
1944	1,401	138	1,539	1,108	15,114
1945	1,293	222	1,515	1,454	14,777
1946	2,374	222	2,596	2,514	19,815
1947	2,376	256	2,632	2,623	22,546
1948	2,292	288	2,580	2,670	23,210

TABLE III—1 (*continued*)

	Convictions for drunkenness			Convictions under Liquor Control Acts	Convictions for all offences
	Male	Female	Total		
J. Alberta (*continued*)					
1949	4,381	275	4,656	3,081	29,124
1950	3,555	294	3,849	3,504	31,993
1951	4,439	252	4,691	3,757	43,858
1952	4,930	211	4,141	6,782	54,338
1953	7,307	446	7,753	5,445	61,633
1954	6,613	426	7,039	5,313	60,192
1955	5,787	488	6,275	5,579	62,490
K. British Columbia					
1881	—	—	225	41	451
1882	—	—	322	43	548
1883	—	—	522	148	1,010
1884	—	—	235	136	485
1885	—	—	108	71	297
1886	—	—	389	120	999
1887	—	—	261	78	732
1888	—	—	370	94	799
1889	—	—	368	89	882
1890	—	—	469	115	1,081
1891	—	—	651	147	1,360
1892	—	—	606	148	1,321
1893	—	—	725	189	1,744
1894	521	60	581	153	1,437
1895	448	50	498	184	1,561
1896	480	100	580	69	1,362
1897	555	75	630	125	1,799
1898	885	80	965	130	2,472
1899	755	80	835	101	2,362
1900	1,114	113	1,227	115	2,994
1901	1,126	106	1,232	156	3,171
1902	1,057	135	1,192	261	3,507
1903	1,239	117	1,356	169	3,602
1904	1,183	105	1,288	133	3,248
1905	1,223	61	1,284	254	3,472
1906	1,631	66	1,697	240	3,952
1907	2,237	56	2,293	382	5,352
1908	2,820	80	2,900	274	6,576
1909	2,261	53	2,314	348	5,248
1910	3,032	5	3,085	436	6,868
1911	5,496	98	5,594	318	11,529
1912	8,174	101	8,275	625	18,125
1913	8,162	154	8,316	741	19,786

TABLE III—1 (*continued*)

	Convictions for drunkenness			Convictions under Liquor Control Acts	Convictions for all offences
	Male	Female	Total		
	K. British Columbia (*continued*)				
1914	9,168	208	9,376	394	22,694
1915	5,799	161	5,960	246	17,673
1916	2,206	121	2,327	295	7,963
1917	2,274	98	2,372	576	8,002
1918	714	64	778	812	7,680
1919	941	63	1,004	597	8,789
1920	2,838	110	2,948	1,427	15,434
1921	2,288	91	2,379	1,394	16,020
1922	1,024	57	1,081	1,503	12,724
1923	1,284	159	1,443	1,196	12,755
1924	1,402	143	1,545	1,286	14,773
1925	1,679	165	1,844	1,699	16,260
1926	1,953	161	2,114	1,345	19,589
1927	2,289	207	2,496	1,186	24,125
1928	2,560	198	2,758	1,350	23,529
1929	2,661	237	2,898	1,556	24,924
1930	2,974	236	3,183	1,432	24,683
1931	2,219	153	2,372	907	21,056
1932	1,120	75	1,195	790	15,220
1933	1,007	61	1,068	782	14,145
1934	1,628	153	1,781	820	16,315
1935	2,090	140	2,230	692	16,847
1936	2,486	248	2,734	965	21,370
1937	2,454	266	2,720	874	26,328
1938	2,828	225	3,053	793	27,138
1939	2,977	249	3,226	1,307	25,582
1940	2,748	256	3,004	903	26,582
1941	2,662	209	2,871	994	31,029
1942	3,683	281	3,964	1,508	27,697
1943	3,686	369	4,055	944	23,602
1944	4,305	439	4,744	1,047	25,284
1945	3,759	583	4,342	1,215	26,367
1946	5,173	801	5,974	2,615	36,119
1947	7,836	965	8,801	1,741	49,710
1948	8,165	970	9,135	1,443	89,375
1949	10,114	1,123	11,237	1,098	98,878
1950	10,278	902	11,180	1,164	122,867
1951	11,770	1,237	13,007	1,251	143,906
1952	12,367	1,112	13,479	1,381	163,778
1953	12,700	1,287	13,987	1,508	166,376
1954	14,882	1,755	16,637	1,557	166,199
1955	14,460	1,754	16,214	1,545	197,393

TABLE III—2

CONVICTIONS FOR DRUNKENNESS, FOR OFFENCES UNDER THE LIQUOR CONTROL ACTS, AND FOR ALL TYPES OF OFFENCE PER 100,000 POPULATION AGED 15 AND OLDER IN CANADA AND PROVINCES, 1881–1955
(For sources and notes, see page 77.)

	Rate of conviction for drunkenness	Rate of conviction for offences under the Liquor Control Acts	Rate of conviction for all offences
		A. Canada	
1881	366	66	1,108
1882	433	63	1,178
1883	474	74	1,236
1884	358	66	1,076
1885	404	74	1,214
1886	394	93	1,202
1887	409	131	1,208
1888	441	146	1,297
1889	469	102	1,301
1890	470	73	1,288
1891	429	75	1,230
1892	371	66	1,135
1893	374	85	1,133
1894	365	67	1,134
1895	361	67	1,162
1896	348	61	1,140
1897	320	63	1,133
1898	328	64	1,111
1899	314	59	1,089
1900	343	54	1,148
1901	351	59	1,165
1902	366	65	1,198
1903	434	77	1,320
1904	487	74	1,396
1905	545	79	1,551
1906	610	78	1,697
1907	701	82	1,861
1908	706	81	2,013
1909	686	88	1,984
1910	729	99	2,204
1911	857	98	2,346
1912	1,077	114	2,966
1913	1,199	117	3,403
1914	1,146	111	3,492
1915	777	103	2,889
1916	617	118	2,335
1917	523	138	2,140
1918	391	139	2,295
1919	443	135	2,378

TABLE III—2 (*continued*)

	Rate of conviction for drunkenness	Rate of conviction for offences under the Liquor Control Acts	Rate of conviction for all offences
A. Canada (*continued*)			
1920	708	182	2,897
1921	597	182	3,076
1922	427	145	2,695
1923	430	170	2,569
1924	452	173	2,632
1925	433	188	2,736
1926	449	215	2,973
1927	482	193	3,283
1928	501	230	4,034
1929	571	284	4,624
1930	515	261	4,855
1931	411	228	5,069
1932	314	169	4,562
1933	258	143	4,440
1934	279	144	4,838
1935	339	116	5,237
1936	369	131	5,377
1937	442	142	5,851
1938	464	156	5,766
1939	446	166	5,905
1940	461	157	6,137
1941	481	185	7,110
1942	531	200	7,366
1943	495	176	5,940
1944	480	196	5,470
1945	535	254	5,701
1946	722	375	7,974
1947	785	314	8,846
1948	771	303	10,052
1949	818	305	11,021
1950	804	337	13,037
1951	858	290	13,831
1952	852	330	16,078
1953	891	341	17,779
1954	907	351	19,501
1955	882	345	20,776
B. Newfoundland			
1951	383	169	2,534
1952	346	209	3,004
1953	452	191	2,987
1954	362	172	3,291
1955	413	232	3,810

TABLE III—2 (*continued*)

	Rate of conviction for drunkenness	Rate of conviction for offences under the Liquor Control Acts	Rate of conviction for all offences
C. Prince Edward Island			
1881	390	75	787
1882	369	115	767
1883	364	79	791
1884	367	115	787
1885	490	134	1,042
1886	528	106	968
1887	403	118	750
1888	422	134	690
1889	485	101	787
1890	422	110	701
1891	457	132	816
1892	443	110	847
1893	343	54	528
1894	256	124	678
1895	242	122	558
1896	193	104	455
1897	436	170	837
1898	430	46	687
1899	485	29	685
1900	488	13	640
1901	360	25	504
1902	348	58	545
1903	422	77	738
1904	443	91	691
1905	265	114	566
1906	185	57	365
1907	225	36	366
1908	292	68	465
1909	254	60	479
1910	290	63	610
1911	378	60	629
1912	490	57	711
1913	514	41	722
1914	534	113	817
1915	367	67	575
1916	353	121	676
1917	339	59	584
1918	160	70	410
1919	193	62	445
1920	200	38	598
1921	240	73	662
1922	270	47	560
1923	278	66	566

TABLE III—2 (*continued*)

	Rate of conviction for drunkenness	Rate of conviction for offences under the Liquor Control Acts	Rate of conviction for all offences
C. Prince Edward Island (*continued*)			
1924	162	50	443
1925	193	88	410
1926	284	90	608
1927	308	112	688
1928	438	115	1,175
1929	677	135	1,397
1930	655	163	1,608
1931	743	87	1,492
1932	582	82	1,480
1933	479	84	1,169
1934	637	127	1,303
1935	731	122	1,512
1936	845	56	1,562
1937	860	255	2,363
1938	888	497	2,570
1939	827	348	2,365
1940	697	321	2,221
1941	817	379	2,835
1942	962	298	2,740
1943	519	184	1,886
1944	617	88	2,420
1945	942	238	2,500
1946	2,239	567	4,598
1947	1,798	536	4,520
1948	1,514	514	4,411
1949	1,702	686	5,075
1950	1,395	412	3,415
1951	1,150	409	3,494
1952	1,543	418	3,929
1953	1,439	400	4,029
1954	1,400	533	4,541
1955	1,455	654	5,177
D. Nova Scotia			
1881	269	17	580
1882	204	7	469
1883	217	21	523
1884	211	18	507
1885	273	22	605
1886	237	21	547
1887	163	25	447
1888	176	29	422
1889	229	31	478

TABLE III—2 (*continued*)

	Rate of conviction for drunkenness	Rate of conviction for offences under the Liquor Control Acts	Rate of conviction for all offences
		D. Nova Scotia (*continued*)	
1890	223	45	514
1891	219	41	510
1892	232	42	556
1893	320	53	667
1894	428	56	833
1895	533	63	1,081
1896	558	65	1,122
1897	404	70	901
1898	426	71	899
1899	340	56	750
1900	414	50	856
1901	456	55	979
1902	664	68	1,280
1903	897	139	1,614
1904	766	121	1,390
1905	824	145	1,504
1906	948	175	1,642
1907	947	156	1,627
1908	881	121	1,615
1909	840	128	1,525
1910	972	153	1,893
1911	966	182	1,745
1912	1,122	167	2,021
1913	1,184	150	2,107
1914	1,180	195	2,177
1915	1,017	187	1,989
1916	1,082	193	1,966
1917	765	135	1,586
1918	733	124	1,660
1919	859	143	1,881
1920	921	116	1,907
1921	623	105	1,610
1922	432	77	1,690
1923	406	77	1,001
1924	424	85	1,152
1925	427	69	995
1926	553	145	1,259
1927	597	177	1,466
1928	631	199	1,562
1929	949	232	2,052
1930	935	154	2,073
1931	618	170	1,881

TABLE III—2 (*continued*)

	Rate of conviction for drunkenness	Rate of conviction for offences under the Liquor Control Acts	Rate of conviction for all offences
D. Nova Scotia (*continued*)			
1932	398	100	1,320
1933	413	164	1,420
1934	408	206	1,431
1935	521	188	1,569
1936	586	184	1,778
1937	668	183	1,899
1938	670	203	1,995
1939	620	297	2,302
1940	893	284	2,651
1941	893	311	2,917
1942	1,047	316	2,872
1943	553	318	2,461
1944	479	519	2,440
1945	703	533	2,730
1946	1,113	805	3,554
1947	1,141	582	3,224
1948	926	526	3,530
1949	1,010	475	3,289
1950	904	504	3,378
1951	1,024	525	3,743
1952	1,246	511	3,721
1953	1,440	479	4,287
1954	1,326	510	4,429
1955	1,438	453	4,683
E. New Brunswick			
1881	574	46	944
1882	687	42	1,563
1883	772	65	1,298
1884	708	92	1,239
1885	653	27	1,027
1886	645	77	1,088
1887	506	114	930
1888	568	110	1,031
1889	688	79	1,117
1890	773	161	1,286
1891	806	121	1,257
1892	636	132	1,117
1893	669	218	1,188
1894	599	164	1,076
1895	588	178	1,088
1896	601	211	1,115

TABLE III—2 (*continued*)

	Rate of conviction for drunkenness	Rate of conviction for offences under the Liquor Control Acts	Rate of conviction for all offences
	E. New Brunswick (*continued*)		
1897	593	164	1,099
1898	620	174	1,132
1899	608	155	1,082
1900	610	143	1,095
1901	610	154	1,076
1902	659	142	1,116
1903	685	138	1,142
1904	780	174	1,277
1905	810	153	1,218
1906	857	144	1,256
1907	917	180	1,356
1908	847	168	1,327
1909	760	158	1,183
1910	697	164	1,158
1911	856	122	1,283
1912	924	158	1,379
1913	886	191	1,421
1914	738	153	1,297
1915	712	164	1,307
1916	719	149	1,254
1917	642	132	1,227
1918	298	122	824
1919	565	162	1,163
1920	759	236	1,548
1921	510	169	1,238
1922	437	147	1,045
1923	431	146	935
1924	469	149	1,085
1925	465	127	1,056
1926	484	154	1,035
1927	544	105	1,097
1928	496	185	1,311
1929	695	186	1,682
1930	651	179	1,689
1931	586	206	1,899
1932	426	182	1,625
1933	413	205	1,451
1934	543	225	1,488
1935	620	200	1,606
1936	757	211	1,881
1937	955	203	2,199
1938	913	163	2,077
1939	719	204	2,047

TABLE III—2 (*continued*)

	Rate of conviction for drunkenness	Rate of conviction for offences under the Liquor Control Acts	Rate of conviction for all offences
	E. New Brunswick (*continued*)		
1940	817	123	2,384
1941	1,068	138	2,849
1942	1,330	150	2,913
1943	1,104	150	2,794
1944	1,363	258	3,442
1945	1,308	286	3,480
1946	2,393	435	4,758
1947	2,013	533	4,750
1948	1,480	385	4,036
1949	1,530	381	4,188
1950	1,491	351	6,823
1951	1,818	246	7,993
1952	1,944	348	9,735
1953	1,968	358	10,008
1954	2,010	282	10,365
1955	1,719	287	11,189
	F. Quebec		
1881	178	48	791
1882	240	62	816
1883	186	77	802
1884	193	38	736
1885	255	52	851
1886	277	57	918
1887	341	69	986
1888	384	72	1,051
1889	386	65	1,082
1890	449	42	1,156
1891	466	48	1,192
1892	421	33	1,152
1893	410	42	1,060
1894	459	30	1,165
1895	458	31	1,207
1896	450	40	1,130
1897	403	42	1,104
1898	388	51	1,031
1899	353	54	1,043
1900	322	46	994
1901	294	45	928
1902	272	59	913
1903	279	63	948
1904	370	54	1,059
1905	440	80	1,282

TABLE III—2 (*continued*)

	Rate of conviction for drunkenness	Rate of conviction for offences under the Liquor Control Acts	Rate of conviction for all offences
F. Quebec (*continued*)			
1906	438	78	1,324
1907	484	62	1,348
1908	585	74	1,587
1909	586	60	1,588
1910	460	74	1,533
1911	551	84	1,602
1912	785	68	2,136
1913	950	61	2,533
1914	965	67	2,579
1915	671	77	2,041
1916	535	76	1,850
1917	599	80	1,937
1918	494	85	2,152
1919	515	107	2,520
1920	835	139	3,103
1921	681	95	3,356
1922	474	64	2,293
1923	410	113	1,979
1924	393	99	1,635
1925	396	120	1,777
1926	328	123	1,679
1927	416	120	1,923
1928	368	121	1,945
1929	470	192	3,155
1930	422	168	3,620
1931	403	160	5,676
1932	309	124	6,268
1933	236	91	6,464
1934	242	118	6,244
1935	236	89	6,409
1936	263	62	5,963
1937	364	66	5,173
1938	341	87	4,704
1939	296	112	4,713
1940	315	95	4,778
1941	365	141	7,221
1942	449	131	8,892
1943	438	87	8,161
1944	369	54	6,544
1945	424	108	6,904
1946	289	93	7,618
1947	436	59	7,776
1948	430	59	9,249

TABLE III—2 (*continued*)

	Rate of conviction for drunkenness	Rate of conviction for offences under the Liquor Control Acts	Rate of conviction for all offences
	F. Quebec (*continued*)		
1949	400	76	9,258
1950	413	118	10,927
1951	380	55	10,249
1952	387	28	11,629
1953	323	46	12,844
1954	369	42	15,700
1955	332	45	15,454
	G. Ontario		
1881	438	81	1,432
1882	457	69	1,439
1883	493	74	1,433
1884	375	80	1,299
1885	462	97	1,581
1886	423	128	1,489
1887	475	204	1,581
1888	501	235	1,737
1889	525	147	1,676
1890	481	83	1,563
1891	359	88	1,401
1892	285	77	1,225
1893	270	96	1,237
1894	231	75	1,183
1895	220	68	1,172
1896	183	52	1,179
1897	171	54	1,179
1898	173	56	1,156
1899	188	52	1,143
1900	227	50	1,241
1901	260	55	1,271
1902	261	52	1,289
1903	330	69	1,438
1904	351	66	1,466
1905	380	54	1,564
1906	466	55	1,721
1907	542	62	1,841
1908	557	67	2,063
1909	584	96	2,134
1910	613	97	2,367
1911	635	98	2,283
1912	704	117	2,675
1913	872	116	3,160

TABLE III—2 (*continued*)

	Rate of conviction for drunkenness	Rate of conviction for offences under the Liquor Control Acts	Rate of conviction for all offences
		G. Ontario (*continued*)	
1914	929	122	3,454
1915	655	105	3,073
1916	615	105	2,603
1917	573	153	2,594
1918	412	177	2,848
1919	435	172	2,726
1920	751	219	3,173
1921	708	241	3,619
1922	482	155	3,353
1923	537	187	3,379
1924	603	217	3,755
1925	537	229	3,963
1926	612	283	4,331
1927	625	245	4,767
1928	680	333	6,640
1929	737	378	6,809
1930	656	369	7,215
1931	502	325	6,690
1932	414	241	5,731
1933	343	199	5,408
1934	350	167	6,679
1935	472	123	7,746
1936	488	157	8,168
1937	589	177	9,294
1938	639	213	9,287
1939	650	185	9,592
1940	630	190	10,064
1941	623	222	10,640
1942	600	235	10,218
1943	590	228	7,461
1944	576	278	7,264
1945	647	352	7,509
1946	962	511	12,161
1947	996	411	13,637
1948	1,050	436	14,462
1949	1,042	422	16,236
1950	1,072	475	10,259
1951	1,149	429	20,497
1952	1,051	435	24,186
1953	1,083	487	27,799
1954	1,070	510	30,176
1955	1,079	499	33,993

TABLE III—2 (*continued*)

	Rate of conviction for drunkenness	Rate of conviction for offences under the Liquor Control Acts	Rate of conviction for all offences
		H. Manitoba	
1881	1,405	411	2,774
1882	3,418	250	5,693
1883	4,608	137	7,029
1884	1,973	96	3,904
1885	1,166	164	2,759
1886	956	120	2,138
1887	735	17	1,238
1888	622	1	971
1889	712	36	1,343
1890	552	17	1,284
1891	551	12	1,061
1892	633	21	1,228
1893	558	57	1,226
1894	518	14	1,041
1895	392	33	996
1896	458	30	1,063
1897	465	40	1,275
1898	418	26	969
1899	442	21	1,034
1900	514	23	1,205
1901	531	38	1,414
1902	590	29	1,336
1903	792	41	1,656
1904	1,253	61	2,690
1905	1,626	39	3,394
1906	1,676	22	3,972
1907	1,819	13	3,791
1908	1,368	28	3,243
1909	1,296	15	3,283
1910	1,489	16	3,481
1911	1,925	15	4,427
1912	2,198	27	4,853
1913	2,278	50	5,500
1914	1,800	48	4,748
1915	1,177	35	3,638
1916	872	48	2,536
1917	302	81	2,272
1918	310	64	2,393
1919	427	48	2,585
1920	618	101	3,320
1921	370	111	3,008

TABLE III—2 *(continued)*

	Rate of conviction for drunkenness	Rate of conviction for offences under the Liquor Control Acts	Rate of conviction for all offences
	H. Manitoba *(continued)*		
1922	415	100	2,741
1923	425	137	3,157
1924	487	113	3,087
1925	479	126	2,933
1926	453	190	3,704
1927	442	147	4,196
1928	422	136	4,896
1929	402	307	6,269
1930	297	252	6,216
1931	226	238	5,349
1932	210	184	4,344
1933	149	144	3,664
1934	166	166	3,927
1935	210	157	3,592
1936	221	185	3,958
1937	203	164	6,062
1938	245	169	6,817
1939	185	197	6,508
1940	284	186	6,401
1941	273	116	6,548
1942	294	210	6,448
1943	351	202	4,478
1944	269	196	4,634
1945	378	265	4,701
1946	502	385	7,261
1947	463	411	9,221
1948	520	353	10,292
1949	659	287	13,609
1950	541	359	14,825
1951	559	354	21,802
1952	579	410	24,355
1953	655	354	24,339
1954	672	432	24,887
1955	614	357	19,343
	I. Saskatchewan		
1907	871	110	2,660
1908	573	53	2,260
1909	511	63	1,962
1910	643	85	2,474
1911	726	74	2,552
1912	716	106	3,024

TABLE III—2 (*continued*)

	Rate of conviction for drunkenness	Rate of conviction for offences under the Liquor Control Acts	Rate of conviction for all offences
	I. Saskatchewan (*continued*)		
1913	811	144	3,642
1914	553	104	3,561
1915	332	94	2,911
1916	259	236	2,687
1917	187	188	1,721
1918	103	100	1,814
1919	143	101	1,697
1920	207	102	1,800
1921	155	128	1,616
1922	175	152	1,778
1923	187	211	2,075
1924	105	200	1,851
1925	135	218	1,958
1926	96	244	2,112
1927	118	238	1,858
1928	187	216	2,002
1929	142	275	2,376
1930	116	240	2,406
1931	78	175	2,253
1932	53	105	1,572
1933	47	91	1,387
1934	50	89	1,317
1935	61	81	1,242
1936	66	91	1,263
1937	68	117	1,695
1938	135	96	1,539
1939	143	95	1,850
1940	92	148	1,937
1941	94	142	2,166
1942	95	164	1,870
1943	131	185	1,685
1944	145	169	1,654
1945	170	238	1,882
1946	312	456	2,785
1947	304	457	2,940
1948	235	390	2,910
1949	256	414	3,112
1950	259	427	4,198
1951	332	345	4,176
1952	388	433	5,706
1953	460	531	6,367
1954	445	581	8,073
1955	520	575	8,037

TABLE III—2 (*continued*)

	Rate of conviction for drunkenness	Rate of conviction for offences under the Liquor Control Acts	Rate of conviction for all offences
		J. Alberta	
1907	947	125	2,905
1908	1,137	153	3,498
1909	1,107	125	3,439
1910	1,575	176	4,229
1911	1,597	167	4,059
1912	2,475	225	6,236
1913	2,538	195	6,769
1914	1,872	181	6,244
1915	884	181	4,549
1916	555	219	3,505
1917	118	267	1,996
1918	243	200	2,252
1919	303	125	2,006
1920	423	170	2,330
1921	490	242	2,626
1922	427	277	2,371
1923	337	261	2,581
1924	383	214	2,556
1925	355	196	2,350
1926	360	188	2,450
1927	288	198	2,502
1928	356	219	2,923
1929	399	224	3,556
1930	327	205	3,255
1931	242	180	3,245
1932	182	111	2,084
1933	115	80	2,400
1934	117	87	2,039
1935	131	89	2,046
1936	146	146	2,229
1937	170	186	2,655
1938	167	146	2,639
1939	203	164	3,208
1940	226	148	3,395
1941	238	229	3,292
1942	251	233	3,196
1943	260	196	2,555
1944	265	191	2,606
1945	262	251	2,552
1946	453	439	3,458
1947	451	449	3,861
1948	429	444	3,862

TABLE III—2 (*continued*)

	Rate of conviction for drunkenness	Rate of conviction for offences under the Liquor Control Acts	Rate of conviction for all offences
J. Alberta (*continued*)			
1949	750	496	4,690
1950	604	550	5,022
1951	718	575	6,716
1952	768	1,014	8,122
1953	1,132	795	8,998
1954	1,001	756	8,562
1955	879	781	8,752
K. British Columbia			
1881	643	117	1,289
1882	826	110	1,405
1883	1,214	344	2,349
1884	511	296	1,054
1885	216	142	594
1886	720	222	1,850
1887	458	137	1,284
1888	607	154	1,310
1889	566	137	1,357
1890	680	167	1,567
1891	892	201	1,863
1892	767	187	1,672
1893	853	222	2,052
1894	638	168	1,579
1895	513	190	1,609
1896	563	67	1,322
1897	578	115	1,650
1898	839	113	2,150
1899	690	83	1,952
1900	966	91	2,357
1901	919	116	2,366
1902	800	175	2,354
1903	822	102	2,183
1904	708	81	1,784
1905	645	128	1,745
1906	804	114	1,873
1907	976	163	2,277
1908	1,155	109	2,620
1909	867	130	1,965
1910	1,090	154	2,427
1911	1,858	112	3,830
1912	2,669	202	5,847
1913	2,599	232	6,183

TABLE III—2 (*continued*)

	Rate of conviction for drunkenness	Rate of conviction for offences under the Liquor Control Acts	Rate of conviction for all offences
K. British Columbia (*continued*)			
1914	2,824	119	6,836
1915	1,779	73	5,276
1916	688	87	2,356
1917	696	169	2,347
1918	225	235	2,220
1919	284	169	2,483
1920	808	391	4,228
1921	634	372	4,272
1922	277	385	3,263
1923	359	298	3,173
1924	371	309	3,551
1925	427	393	3,764
1926	473	301	4,382
1927	540	257	5,224
1928	578	283	4,933
1929	589	316	5,066
1930	628	282	4,868
1931	454	173	4,026
1932	223	147	2,840
1933	195	143	2,586
1934	319	147	2,924
1935	391	121	2,956
1936	467	165	3,647
1937	456	149	4,493
1938	500	130	4,449
1939	517	210	4,100
1940	473	142	4,186
1941	447	155	4,826
1942	582	221	4,067
1943	578	135	3,367
1944	657	145	5,019
1945	592	166	3,597
1946	775	339	4,685
1947	1,106	219	6,245
1948	1,113	176	10,886
1949	1,343	131	11,813
1950	1,317	137	14,472
1951	1,511	145	16,714
1952	1,537	157	18,675
1953	1,570	169	18,673
1954	1,828	171	18,264
1955	1,745	166	21,248

TABLE III—3

CONVICTIONS FOR KEEPING OR OPERATING AN ILLICIT STILL IN CANADA AND PROVINCES, 1920–1955
(For sources and notes, see page 78.)

	Canada	New-foundland	P.E.I.	Nova Scotia	New Brunswick	Quebec	Ontario	Manitoba	Saskatchewan	Alberta	B.C.
1920	239	—	—	—	—	26	67	8	73	52	13
1921	220	—	—	1	14	81	59	15	31	12	7
1922	643	—	—	20	38	115	245	51	121	46	7
1923	1,068	—	6	6	12	281	339	42	244	132	12
1924	953	—	0	0	23	187	300	50	300	83	4
1925	548	—	0	1	5	127	155	12	187	54	7
1926	376	—	0	1	2	76	117	29	98	49	4
1927	353	—	5	1	3	136	100	25	65	18	5
1928	291	—	1	5	1	104	53	34	51	29	9
1929	280	—	0	1	0	69	40 †	47	77	37	8
1930	345	—	0	3	0	93	40	86	94	18	11
1931	428	—	0	7	4	133	81	47	106	26	24
1932	435	—	0	11	2	181	132	45	31	16	17
1933	459	—	0	10	1	151	174	18	46	45	14
1934	419	—	0	5	1	143	117	5	63	78	7
1935	247	—	0	5	0	116	46	19	22	40	4
1936	355	—	0	0	0	103	68	29	55	75	5
1937	460	—	2	0	1	81	59	63	106	137	12
1938	440	—	13	1	1	72	48	114	88	101	13
1939	324	—	2	13	0	60	42	49	95	45	7
1940	444	—	5	20	6	91	40	101	122	51	11
1941	325	—	6	5	17	74	24	41	119	27	13
1942	181	—	19	14	4	26	22	55	27	24	3
1943	116	—	1	12	2	7	11	23	26	9	7
1944	172	—	25	6	0	33	25	41	45	11	10
1945	278	—	9	45	2	120	25	19	35	6	1
1946	172	—	4	4	1	61	32	42	15	7	1
1947	82	—	0	18	0	11	17	17	15	0	0
1948	77	—	0	4	0	30	3	32	7	1	0
1949	49	—	0	1	0	3	12	18	7	8	0
1950	13	—	0	6	0	7	0	0	0	0	0
1951	23	0	1	3	0	0	1	15	2	2	0
1952	17	0	0	1	0	0	2	13	1	0	0
1953	2	0	0	0	1	1	0	1	0	0	0
1954	2	0	0	1	0	0	0	0	0	0	0
1955	0	0	0	0	0	0	0	0	0	0	0

TABLE III—4

CONVICTIONS FOR DRUNKEN DRIVING, NUMBER OF REGISTERED MOTOR VEHICLES, AND DRUNKEN DRIVING CONVICTIONS PER 100,000 REGISTERED VEHICLES IN CANADA AND PROVINCES, 1924-1955

(For sources and notes, see page 78.)

	Canada			Newfoundland			Prince Edward I.		
	Convictions for drunken driving	Number of motor vehicles	Convictions per 100,000 vehicles	Convictions for drunken driving	Number of motor vehicles	Convictions per 100,000 vehicles	Convictions for drunken driving	Number of motor vehicles	Convictions per 100,000 vehicles
1924	529	645,151	82	—	—	—	2	2,571	78
1925	609	723,936	84	—	—	—	0	2,947	0
1926	724	832,128	87	—	—	—	1	3,448	29
1927	953	939,483	101	—	—	—	9	4,371	206
1928	1,322	1,069,146	124	—	—	—	13	5,404	241
1929	2,105	1,187,112	177	—	—	—	19	6,116	311
1930	1,799	1,232,258	146	—	—	—	23	7,376	312
1931	1,397	1,200,444	116	—	—	—	21	7,744	271
1932	952	1,113,301	86	—	—	—	12	6,982	172
1933	744	1,082,949	69	—	—	—	22	6,940	317
1934	835	1,129,284	74	—	—	—	15	7,206	208
1935	1,149	1,175,853	98	—	—	—	29	8,231	352
1936	1,018	1,239,824	82	—	—	—	11	7,632	144
1937	1,439	1,319,373	109	—	—	—	37	8,011	462
1938	1,877	1,394,511	135	—	—	—	43	7,992	538
1939	1,735	1,438,874	121	—	—	—	55	8,040	684
1940	1,794	1,500,422	120	—	—	—	42	8,070	520
1941	1,982	1,572,357	126	—	—	—	37	8,015	462
1942	1,720	1,523,731	113	—	—	—	24	7,537	318
1943	1,265	1,511,305	84	—	—	—	21	8,032	261
1944	1,151	1,501,809	77	—	—	—	23	8,412	273
1945	1,268	1,496,467	85	—	—	—	30	8,835	340
1946	1,892	1,621,182	117	—	—	—	71	9,192	772
1947	1,820	1,834,173	99	—	—	—	50	9,948	503
1948	1,980	2,032,452	97	—	—	—	55	11,290	487
1949	2,679	2,288,084	117	—	—	—	55	13,211	416
1950	3,073	2,597,287	118	—	—	—	43	15,383	280
1951	5,831	2,869,039	203	126	20,058	628	74	16,896	438
1952	1,898	3,151,741	60	65	23,630	275	0	18,717	0
1953	2,895	3,426,112	84	66	29,576	223	12	20,286	59
1954	2,515	3,639,606	69	116	34,423	337	24	20,848	115
1955	2,389	3,943,541	61	118	39,766	297	35	22,145	158

TABLE III—4 (continued)

	Nova Scotia			New Brunswick			Quebec		
	Convictions for drunken driving	Number of motor vehicles	Convictions per 100,000 vehicles	Convictions for drunken driving	Number of motor vehicles	Convictions per 100,000 vehicles	Convictions for drunken driving	Number of motor vehicles	Convictions per 100,000 vehicles
1924	3	20,606	15	11	19,840	55	119	84,949	140
1925	7	22,745	31	14	18,863	74	117	97,418	120
1926	6	25,746	23	13	21,421	61	173	107,994	160
1927	19	29,914	64	27	24,457	110	156	128,104	122
1928	26	35,194	74	36	27,970	129	174	148,090	117
1929	39	39,972	98	60	31,736	189	335	169,105	198
1930	36	43,029	84	66	34,699	190	360	178,548	202
1931	48	43,758	110	7	33,627	21	273	177,485	154
1932	29	41,013	71	71	28,041	253	142	165,730	86
1933	30	40,648	74	45	26,867	167	156	160,012	97
1934	44	41,932	105	53	29,094	182	193	165,526	117
1935	55	43,952	125	78	31,217	250	198	170,644	116
1936	88	46,179	191	85	33,402	254	157	181,628	86
1937	80	50,048	160	102	36,780	277	159	197,917	80
1938	102	51,214	199	106	37,110	286	224	205,463	109
1939	138	53,008	260	67	38,116	176	179	213,148	84
1940	153	57,873	264	106	39,000	272	156	225,152	69
1941	193	62,805	311	153	41,450	369	174	232,149	75
1942	143	58,872	243	101	37,758	267	208	222,622	93
1943	83	59,194	140	74	40,205	184	147	222,676	66
1944	110	57,933	190	116	39,570	293	102	224,042	46
1945	88	56,699	155	142	41,577	342	106	228,681	46
1946	165	62,660	263	159	44,654	356	101	255,172	40
1947	198	70,300	282	155	51,589	300	110	296,547	37
1948	149	76,319	195	228	62,366	366	120	335,953	36
1949	191	83,443	229	297	67,280	441	261	384,733	68
1950	205	94,743	216	260	74,415	349	340	433,701	78
1951	345	105,262	328	369	83,023	444	484	500,729	97
1952	94	114,982	82	120	89,839	134	160	574,974	28
1953	307	129,564	237	125	93,914	133	596	617,855	96
1954	181	133,087	136	136	99,058	137	344	674,114	51
1955	179	149,841	119	93	106,648	87	280	743,682	38

TABLE III—4 (continued)

	Ontario			Manitoba			Saskatchewan		
	Convictions for drunken driving	Number of motor vehicles	Convictions per 100,000 vehicles	Convictions for drunken driving	Number of motor vehicles	Convictions per 100,000 vehicles	Convictions for drunken driving	Number of motor vehicles	Convictions per 100,000 vehicles
1924	230	306,770	75	104	43,875	237	6	69,895	9
1925	321	342,174	94	74	50,884	145	18	77,940	23
1926	358	386,349	93	67	58,292	115	40	95,967	42
1927	578	433,504	133	70	63,412	110	46	105,088	44
1928	768	487,337	158	155	70,578	220	38	119,972	32
1929	966	540,207	179	437	77,259	566	75	128,426	58
1930	969	562,506	172	123	78,850	156	55	127,193	43
1931	736	562,216	131	104	75,210	138	44	107,830	41
1932	554	531,597	104	71	70,840	100	18	91,275	20
1933	386	520,353	74	64	68,590	93	9	84,944	11
1934	431	542,245	79	35	70,430	50	12	91,461	13
1935	617	564,076	109	86	70,660	122	27	94,792	28
1936	498	590,226	84	80	74,940	107	23	102,270	22
1937	824	623,918	132	88	80,860	109	31	105,064	30
1938	1,101	669,088	165	100	88,219	113	33	109,014	30
1939	998	682,891	146	85	88,864	96	54	119,018	45
1940	1,021	703,872	145	128	90,932	141	70	126,970	55
1941	1,117	739,194	151	114	96,573	118	55	131,545	42
1942	967	715,380	135	110	93,147	118	57	130,040	44
1943	730	691,615	106	93	93,494	99	40	133,839	30
1944	618	675,057	92	74	93,297	79	44	140,992	31
1945	641	662,719	97	83	92,297	90	62	140,257	44
1946	1,057	711,106	149	122	101,090	121	89	148,206	60
1947	1,009	800,058	126	108	112,149	96	64	158,512	40
1948	1,070	874,933	122	121	128,000	95	61	167,515	36
1949	1,249	970,137	129	173	139,836	124	113	185,027	61
1950	1,588	1,104,080	144	191	157,546	121	95	199,866	48
1951	2,822	1,205,098	234	324	171,265	189	179	215,450	83
1952	1,174	1,291,753	91	193	187,881	103	18	237,014	8
1953	1,295	1,406,119	92	222	203,652	109	73	257,504	28
1954	1,232	1,489,980	83	252	210,471	120	56	267,373	21
1955	1,229	1,617,853	76	212	222,474	95	60	274,950	22

TABLE III—4 (continued)

	Alberta			British Columbia		
	Convictions for drunken driving	Number of motor vehicles	Convictions per 100,000 vehicles	Convictions for drunken driving	Number of motor vehicles	Convictions per 100,000 vehicles
1924	25	48,238	52	29	48,407	60
1925	42	54,538	77	16	56,427	28
1926	54	65,101	83	12	67,810	18
1927	25	73,306	34	23	77,327	30
1928	76	88,398	86	36	86,203	42
1929	94	98,720	95	80	95,571	84
1930	95	101,119	94	72	98,938	73
1931	46	94,642	49	58	97,932	59
1932	24	86,781	28	31	91,042	34
1933	19	86,041	22	13	88,554	15
1934	15	89,369	17	37	92,021	40
1935	27	93,870	29	32	98,411	33
1936	26	97,460	27	50	106,079	47
1937	45	100,434	45	73	116,341	63
1938	59	107,191	55	109	119,220	91
1939	63	113,702	55	96	122,087	79
1940	55	120,514	46	53	128,044	41
1941	58	126,127	46	81	134,499	60
1942	46	125,482	37	64	132,893	48
1943	49	127,559	38	28	134,691	21
1944	33	127,416	26	31	135,090	23
1945	85	130,150	65	31	134,788	23
1946	72	138,868	52	56	150,234	37
1947	67	155,386	43	59	179,684	33
1948	69	173,950	40	107	202,126	53
1949	132	200,428	66	208	230,008	90
1950	138	230,624	60	213	270,312	79
1951	608	259,841	234	500	291,417	172
1952	60	291,469	21	14	321,482	4
1953	107	318,812	34	92	348,830	26
1954	140	338,514	41	34	371,711	9
1955	134	356,839	38	49	409,343	12

TABLE III—5

CONVICTIONS FOR IMPAIRED DRIVING IN CANADA AND PROVINCES, 1952–1955
(For sources and notes, see page 78.)

	Can.	Nfld.	P.E.I.	N.S.	N.B.	Que.	Ont.	Man.	Sask.	Alta.	B.C.
1952	10,182	144	160	393	477	1,325	4,471	529	478	810	1,395
1953	13,920	145	229	364	689	2,079	5,518	627	700	1,224	2,345
1954	14,294	157	163	410	426	2,473	5,919	593	672	1,019	2,462
1955	15,188	202	182	627	698	2,937	6,244	555	638	1,116	1,990

TABLE III—6

IMPAIRED DRIVING CONVICTIONS PER 100,000 REGISTERED MOTOR VEHICLES IN CANADA AND PROVINCES, 1952 1955
(For sources and notes, see page 78.)

	Can.	Nfld.	P.E.I.	N.S.	N.B.	Que.	Ont.	Man.	Sask.	Alta.	B.C.
1952	323	609	855	342	531	230	346	282	202	278	434
1953	406	490	1,129	281	734	336	392	308	272	321	672
1954	393	456	782	308	430	367	397	282	251	301	662
1955	385	508	822	418	654	395	386	249	232	313	426

TABLE III—7

CONVICTIONS FOR DRUNKENNESS, AND FOR OFFENCES UNDER THE LIQUOR CONTROL ACTS PER 100,000 POPULATION AGED 15 AND OLDER; AND CONVICTIONS FOR DRUNKEN AND IMPAIRED DRIVING IN CANADA AND PROVINCES, 1955
(For sources and notes, see page 78.)

	Rate of conviction for drunkenness	Rate of conviction for offences under Liquor Control Acts	Convictions for drunken driving per 100,000 vehicles	Convictions for impaired driving per 100,000 vehicles
Canada	882	345	61	385
Newfoundland	413	232	297	508
Prince Edward Island	1,455	654	158	822
Nova Scotia	1,438	453	119	418
New Brunswick	1,719	287	87	654
Quebec	332	45	38	395
Ontario	1,079	499	76	386
Manitoba	614	357	95	249
Saskatchewan	520	575	22	232
Alberta	879	781	38	313
British Columbia	1,745	166	12	486

SOURCES AND NOTES

Table III—1, A-K

All provincial figures were obtained from the *Annual Reports on Statistics of Criminal and Other Offences* (Ottawa: Dominion Bureau of Statistics). The figures shown for Canada represent the total of available provincial figures in each year, and are exclusive of the Yukon and Northwest Territories throughout, of Saskatchewan and Alberta until 1907, and of Newfoundland until 1951. From 1881 to 1950, all figures apply to the year ending September 30; from 1951 to 1955, inclusive, figures apply to the calendar year. Prior to 1922, convictions of persons under 16 years of age could not be excluded from the data; from 1922 to 1955, inclusive, such convictions were separately reported by the Dominion Bureau under the category of "juvenile delinquents," and, accordingly, were excluded from the data shown for these years.

Prior to 1953, all convictions for drunkenness were listed solely under "intoxication" in the *Reports* of the Dominion Bureau; from 1953 to 1955, inclusive, such convictions were listed under: (1) Indian Act—Intoxication; (2) Liquor Control Act—Intoxication; and (3) Intoxication. The figures shown for this period represent the sum of the convictions reported under these three categories in each year.

Convictions for offences under the Liquor Control Acts are exclusive of convictions for drunkenness in all cases. These offences include all other violations of: (1) the provincial Liquor Control Acts; (2) the provincial Liquor Licence Acts; (3) the Canada Temperance Act; and (4) liquor laws under the Indian Act.

The conviction figures shown for all offences include convictions for drunkenness, and for offences under the Liquor Control Acts, as well as total convictions for all other types of offence: both indictable and non-indictable.

When differences from year to year, or from province to province in the number of convictions for a particular offence are under consideration, it should be kept in mind that several factors may be responsible other than, or in addition to variation in the prevalence of persons who commit such an offence. Thus, for example: (1) Figures represent number of convictions and not numbers of individuals convicted. Therefore, account should be taken of the possibility that some individuals may be convicted more than once for the same offence in any given year. (2) Differences in the number of sub-areas reporting data to the Dominion Bureau from one year to another, or from province to province may lead to corresponding differences in number of reported convictions. (3) An alteration in the existing legal definition of an offence, or variation in definition from one province to another may be reflected in differences in the number of convictions reported for the offence. (4) Both temporal and inter-provincial differences may be dependent, to varying degrees, on differences in the definition of the offence employed in practice by law enforcement agencies, and, perhaps ultimately, on differences in community attitudes towards the activity in question. Such factors may be of particular significance in the case of convictions for drunkenness.

Table III—2, A-K

Rates were based on the conviction data provided in Table III—1, A-K, and the population figures for the age group of 15 and older shown in Table V—1, A-K. The conviction data for the years 1922 to 1955, inclusive, applied solely to persons aged 16 and older. However, the group aged 15 and older represented the nearest approximation for which intercensal estimates were available. Some error was presumably

77

also introduced into rate estimates for the years prior to 1922, through the use of this age group, since convictions of persons under 16 years of age could not be excluded from the basic conviction data for these years (see notes to Table III—1, A-K). However, while this factor may appreciably affect the accuracy of the conviction rates for all types of offence, its effect on the accuracy of the rates of drunkenness, and offences under the Liquor Control Acts is probably negligible. Thus, relatively few convictions for such offences would be expected among persons under 16 years of age.

Table III—3

All provincial figures were obtained from the *Annual Reports on Statistics of Criminal and Other Offences* (Ottawa: Dominion Bureau of Statistics). The figures shown for Canada represent the total of available provincial figures in each year and are exclusive of the Yukon and Northwest Territories throughout, of Nova Scotia and New Brunswick until 1921, Prince Edward Island until 1924, and Newfoundland until 1951. With the exception of the latter province, convictions for this offence were not separately reported prior to the earliest year shown in each case, but were included in the category of "Offences under the Revenue Laws." No data were available for Newfoundland in Dominion Bureau reports prior to 1951.

Table III—4

All provincial data on convictions for drunken driving were obtained from the *Annual Reports on Statistics of Criminal and Other Offences* (Ottawa: Dominion Bureau of Statistics); the data on numbers of registered motor vehicles were obtained from the *Annual Reports on the Motor Vehicle* (Ottawa: Dominion Bureau of Statistics). The figures shown for Canada represent the total of available provincial figures in each year, and are exclusive of the Yukon and Northwest Territories throughout, and of Newfoundland until 1951.

Convictions for drunken driving were first listed in Dominion Bureau reports under "summary convictions." In 1937 drunken driving was changed to an indictable offence, and the listing was changed accordingly. In 1951, the Criminal Code was amended, making it an offence to have care or control of a motor vehicle while the ability was impaired by alcohol. This was a new offence and did not replace the older one of drunken driving. Convictions for "impaired driving" were not separately reported until 1952. However, it is important to note that convictions for this offence took place during 1951, and are included in the figures for drunken driving shown for that year.

The category "registered motor vehicles" includes passenger cars, commercial vehicles, and motorcycles.

Table III—5

All provincial figures were obtained from the *Annual Reports on Statistics of Criminal and Other Offences*. The figures shown for Canada represent the sum of the ten provincial figures in each year.

See also notes to Table III—4.

Table III—6

Rates were based on the conviction data shown in Table III—5, and appropriate motor vehicle figures provided in Table III—4.

Table III—7

The sources of the various rates included in this summary table maybe found in the notes to Table III—2, A-K; Table III—4; and Table III—6.

PART IV

Statistics Relating to the Prevalence of Alcoholism

TABLE IV—1

(For sources and notes, see page 121.)

	Alcoholism deaths			Liver cirrhosis deaths		
	Total	Male	Female	Total	Male	Female
			A. Canada			
1921	116	108	8	291	172	119
1922	99	96	3	282	172	110
1923	136	122	14	331	195	136
1924	147	134	13	278	162	116
1925	148	137	11	385	230	155
1926	208	186	22	283	174	109
1927	229	213	16	347	228	119
1928	221	202	19	363	224	139
1929	247	224	23	367	213	154
1930	186	167	19	333	204	129
1931	146	137	9	367	227	140
1932	136	122	14	394	235	159
1933	98	83	15	365	211	154
1934	120	109	11	394	232	162
1935	159	144	15	416	261	155
1936	185	168	17	453	277	176
1937	205	191	14	405	259	146
1938	163	148	15	483	301	182
1939	122	106	16	500	312	188
1940	150	138	12	460	290	170
1941	83	73	10	474	282	192
1942	59	50	9	563	340	223
1943	57	50	7	524	334	190
1944	66	61	5	502	305	197
1945	75	67	8	558	352	206
1946	91	74	17	596	390	206
1947	84	72	12	628	415	213
1948	83	71	12	656	416	240
1949	74	64	10	761	482	279
1950	—	—	—	615	387	228
1951	—	—	—	607	386	221
1952	—	—	—	652	403	249
1953	—	—	—	726	458	268
1954	—	—	—	742	469	273
1955	—	—	—	756	507	249
1956	—	—	—	835	550	285

81

TABLE IV—1 (*continued*)

	Alcoholism deaths			Liver cirrhosis deaths		
	Total	Male	Female	Total	Male	Female
B. Newfoundland						
1949	—	—	—	4	4	0
1950	—	—	—	3	3	0
1951	—	—	—	2	1	1
1952	—	—	—	4	3	1
1953	—	—	—	8	4	4
1954	—	—	—	5	4	1
1955	—	—	—	11	8	3
1956	—	—	—	5	4	1
C. Prince Edward Island						
1921	1	1	0	3	1	2
1922	0	0	0	1	1	0
1923	2	1	1	1	0	1
1924	1	1	0	1	0	1
1925	0	0	0	6	3	3
1926	3	3	0	1	1	0
1927	0	0	0	1	0	1
1928	0	0	0	0	0	0
1929	1	1	0	3	1	2
1930	2	2	0	2	0	2
1931	0	0	0	0	0	0
1932	0	0	0	3	3	0
1933	0	0	0	2	2	0
1934	1	1	0	3	1	2
1935	1	1	0	2	1	1
1936	3	3	0	1	1	0
1937	4	4	0	3	0	3
1938	0	0	0	0	0	0
1939	2	1	1	4	2	2
1940	2	2	0	0	0	0
1941	0	0	0	4	3	1
1942	0	0	0	3	3	0
1943	0	0	0	5	5	0
1944	3	1	2	2	1	1
1945	1	1	0	4	4	0
1946	1	0	1	5	2	3
1947	1	1	0	2	2	0
1948	1	1	0	0	0	0
1949	0	0	0	6	3	3
1950	—	—	—	4	3	1
1951	—	—	—	4	2	2
1952	—	—	—	2	1	1

TABLE IV—1 (*continued*)

	Alcoholism deaths			Liver cirrhosis deaths		
	Total	Male	Female	Total	Male	Female
C. Prince Edward Island (*continued*)						
1953	—	—	—	0	0	0
1954	—	—	—	4	2	2
1955	—	—	—	4	2	2
1956	—	—	—	3	3	0
D. Nova Scotia						
1909	11	—	—	24	—	—
1910	7	—	—	15	—	—
1911	5	—	—	10	—	—
1912	8	—	—	25	—	—
1913	15	—	—	18	—	—
1914	14	—	—	20	—	—
1915	9	—	—	22	—	—
1916	—	—	—	—	—	—
1917	9	—	—	6	—	—
1918	4	—	—	18	—	—
1919	7	—	—	7	—	—
1920	7	—	—	11	—	—
1921	6	5	1	11	8	3
1922	8	7	1	13	9	4
1923	4	4	0	13	8	5
1924	6	6	0	9	2	7
1925	11	11	0	12	9	3
1926	6	6	0	15	12	3
1927	8	8	0	15	7	8
1928	18	18	0	9	6	3
1929	8	8	0	13	6	7
1930	15	15	0	12	8	4
1931	5	5	0	16	13	3
1932	5	5	0	13	9	4
1933	3	3	0	14	11	3
1934	13	13	0	21	13	8
1935	13	13	0	12	12	0
1936	8	8	0	17	10	7
1937	12	12	0	8	5	3
1938	4	4	0	13	8	5
1939	6	5	1	20	14	6
1940	6	6	0	19	11	8
1941	8	8	0	13	5	8
1942	3	2	1	19	13	6
1943	5	5	0	16	6	10
1944	2	2	0	13	8	5

TABLE IV—1 (*continued*)

	Alcoholism deaths			Liver cirrhosis deaths		
	Total	Male	Female	Total	Male	Female

D. Nova Scotia (*continued*)

1945	5	5	0	22	13	9
1946	9	8	1	14	10	4
1947	6	5	1	17	7	10
1948	7	7	0	26	13	13
1949	3	3	0	20	13	7
1950	—	—	—	16	10	6
1951	—	—	—	16	8	8
1952	—	—	—	24	13	11
1953	—	—	—	26	14	12
1954	—	—	—	30	17	13
1955	—	—	—	24	15	9
1956	—	—	—	23	12	11

E. New Brunswick

1921	3	3	0	13	11	2
1922	2	1	1	5	1	4
1923	9	9	0	10	5	5
1924	5	5	0	4	2	2
1925	8	8	0	14	4	10
1926	4	4	0	11	6	5
1927	9	9	0	11	8	3
1928	2	2	0	9	8	1
1929	18	15	3	8	6	2
1930	4	4	0	13	10	3
1931	7	7	0	7	4	3
1932	5	4	1	10	9	1
1933	6	6	0	9	4	5
1934	8	8	0	7	2	5
1935	7	5	2	12	9	3
1936	17	16	1	12	9	3
1937	11	11	0	6	4	2
1938	9	8	1	14	8	6
1939	3	3	0	18	12	6
1940	12	10	2	13	5	8
1941	4	4	0	7	5	2
1942	1	1	0	11	5	6
1943	3	3	0	14	4	10
1944	5	4	1	5	2	3
1945	6	6	0	10	4	6
1946	7	7	0	11	8	3
1947	6	5	1	14	10	4
1948	7	7	0	13	4	9
1949	10	10	0	22	12	10

TABLE IV—1 (*continued*)

	Alcoholism deaths			Liver cirrhosis deaths		
	Total	Male	Female	Total	Male	Female
E. New Brunswick (*continued*)						
1950	—	—	—	15	11	4
1951	—	—	—	9	4	5
1952	—	—	—	20	9	11
1953	—	—	—	14	7	7
1954	—	—	—	18	13	5
1955	—	—	—	14	9	5
1956	—	—	—	20	12	8
F. Quebec						
1901	20	—	—	73	—	—
1902	21	—	—	68	—	—
1903	36	—	—	101	—	—
1904	47	—	—	94	—	—
1905	27	—	—	105	—	—
1906	47	—	—	103	—	—
1907	55	—	—	134	—	—
1908	48	—	—	96	—	—
1909	39	—	—	127	—	—
1910	38	—	—	121	—	—
1911	52	—	—	134	—	—
1912	49	—	—	159	—	—
1913	63	—	—	168	—	—
1914	44	—	—	161	—	—
1915	44	—	—	143	—	—
1916	55	—	—	161	—	—
1917	49	—	—	153	—	—
1918	59	—	—	166	—	—
1919	35	—	—	133	—	—
1920	35	—	—	133	—	—
1921	34	30	4	147	81	66
1922	7	7	0	123	76	47
1923	13	12	1	153	90	63
1924	22	20	2	114	60	54
1925	20	17	3	171	97	74
1926	52	49	3	125	69	56
1927	57	52	5	132	86	46
1928	47	43	4	168	106	62
1929	32	28	4	168	87	81
1930	33	28	5	159	96	63
1931	36	31	5	182	108	74
1932	26	23	3	187	107	80
1933	13	9	4	154	83	71
1934	24	22	2	179	103	76

TABLE IV—1 (*continued*)

	Alcoholism deaths			Liver cirrhosis deaths		
	Total	Male	Female	Total	Male	Female
F. Quebec (*continued*)						
1935	46	41	5	184	108	76
1936	51	46	5	210	116	94
1937	66	62	4	181	113	68
1938	45	40	5	192	122	70
1939	38	35	3	191	117	74
1940	51	48	3	181	122	59
1941	18	16	2	192	112	80
1942	14	12	2	225	131	94
1943	12	8	4	220	139	81
1944	20	20	0	207	123	84
1945	9	8	1	222	136	86
1946	18	18	0	230	150	80
1947	21	21	0	213	150	63
1948	15	15	0	201	128	73
1949	20	16	4	245	158	87
1950	—	—	—	200	127	73
1951	—	—	—	194	122	72
1952	—	—	—	189	126	63
1953	—	—	—	211	137	74
1954	—	—	—	204	137	67
1955	—	—	—	234	168	66
1956	—	—	—	255	183	72
G. Ontario						
1901	18	—	—	—	—	—
1902	24	—	—	—	—	—
1903	24	—	—	—	—	—
1904	28	—	—	—	—	—
1905	38	—	—	—	—	—
1906	42	—	—	—	—	—
1907	55	—	—	93	—	—
1908	71	—	—	92	—	—
1909	83	—	—	98	—	—
1910	69	—	—	104	—	—
1911	98	—	—	122	—	—
1912	149	—	—	103	—	—
1913	118	—	—	121	—	—
1914	89	—	—	115	—	—
1915	67	—	—	100	—	—
1916	56	—	—	120	—	—
1917	55	—	—	105	—	—
1918	40	—	—	64	—	—
1919	40	—	—	69	—	—

TABLE IV—1 (*continued*)

	Alcoholism deaths			Liver cirrhosis deaths		
	Total	Male	Female	Total	Male	Female
			G. Ontario (*continued*)			
1920	63	—	—	93	—	—
1921	40	39	1	80	43	37
1922	41	41	0	91	52	39
1923	61	55	6	99	60	39
1924	49	45	4	83	46	37
1925	56	50	6	112	70	42
1926	86	75	11	75	47	28
1927	83	76	7	125	82	43
1928	73	67	6	104	58	46
1929	93	87	6	112	68	44
1930	74	66	8	88	45	43
1931	51	48	3	107	66	41
1932	67	61	6	115	66	49
1933	48	42	6	110	64	46
1934	46	40	6	122	70	52
1935	58	52	6	117	71	46
1936	62	55	7	119	84	35
1937	63	57	6	129	82	47
1938	58	54	4	154	89	65
1939	44	36	8	156	95	61
1940	45	42	3	154	96	58
1941	27	23	4	146	83	63
1942	21	17	4	170	105	65
1943	22	20	2	151	98	53
1944	29	27	2	148	93	55
1945	33	30	3	162	112	50
1946	35	25	10	177	111	66
1947	31	25	6	220	141	79
1948	36	27	9	224	144	80
1949	24	20	4	260	162	98
1950	—	—	—	243	146	97
1951	—	—	—	217	137	80
1952	—	—	—	239	146	93
1953	—	—	—	270	175	95
1954	—	—	—	289	179	110
1955	—	—	—	292	197	95
1956	—	—	—	310	189	121
			H. Manitoba			
1921	10	9	1	6	5	1
1922	3	3	0	8	6	2
1923	9	8	1	12	7	5
1924	14	13	1	15	9	6

TABLE IV—1 (*continued*)

	Alcoholism deaths			Liver cirrhosis deaths		
	Total	Male	Female	Total	Male	Female
H. Manitoba (*continued*)						
1925	9	8	1	12	5	7
1926	15	15	0	13	11	2
1927	24	24	0	14	8	6
1928	19	16	3	17	8	9
1929	22	20	2	9	7	2
1930	6	5	1	12	9	3
1931	11	10	1	10	6	4
1932	8	7	1	14	9	5
1933	4	2	2	18	13	5
1934	8	6	2	20	11	9
1935	6	5	1	24	15	9
1936	12	10	2	22	12	10
1937	12	10	2	14	10	4
1938	6	5	1	26	18	8
1939	6	5	1	27	16	11
1940	5	4	1	18	13	5
1941	8	5	3	33	19	14
1942	8	6	2	28	18	10
1943	2	2	0	27	18	9
1944	1	1	0	27	17	10
1945	9	7	2	28	16	12
1946	3	3	0	31	21	10
1947	4	2	2	16	10	6
1948	0	0	0	40	27	13
1949	3	1	2	31	17	14
1950	—	—	—	28	15	13
1951	—	—	—	26	15	11
1952	—	—	—	28	16	12
1953	—	—	—	35	16	19
1954	—	—	—	37	19	18
1955	—	—	—	34	18	16
1956	—	—	—	41	31	10
I. Saskatchewan						
1921	2	2	0	11	8	3
1922	11	11	0	13	8	5
1923	11	11	0	15	9	6
1924	8	8	0	12	8	4
1925	13	13	0	21	13	8
1926	8	8	0	16	11	5
1927	15	13	2	10	9	1
1928	14	14	0	14	7	7

TABLE IV—1 (*continued*)

	Alcoholism deaths			Liver cirrhosis deaths		
	Total	Male	Female	Total	Male	Female
I. Saskatchewan (*continued*)						
1929	14	13	1	8	4	4
1930	15	14	1	16	14	2
1931	8	8	0	18	9	9
1932	3	3	0	12	5	7
1933	3	2	1	13	5	8
1934	7	7	0	6	6	0
1935	3	3	0	22	14	8
1936	2	2	0	22	9	13
1937	7	7	0	19	8	11
1938	10	10	0	22	14	8
1939	3	3	0	23	14	9
1940	6	5	1	17	8	9
1941	5	5	0	21	13	8
1942	2	2	0	28	18	10
1943	1	1	0	22	14	8
1944	1	1	0	30	17	13
1945	4	3	1	28	18	10
1946	2	1	1	30	20	10
1947	3	3	0	27	11	16
1948	1	1	0	30	20	10
1949	0	0	0	38	18	20
1950	—	—	—	30	22	8
1951	—	—	—	22	13	9
1952	—	—	—	26	17	9
1953	—	—	—	29	17	12
1954	—	—	—	29	18	11
1955	—	—	—	23	14	9
1956	—	—	—	25	17	8
J. Alberta						
1921	9	9	0	8	6	2
1922	12	11	1	10	5	5
1923	13	11	2	9	4	5
1924	15	12	3	15	14	1
1925	10	10	0	10	6	4
1926	11	9	2	9	6	3
1927	11	9	2	16	11	5
1928	21	17	4	14	10	4
1929	18	16	2	12	7	5
1930	6	6	0	12	7	5
1931	12	12	0	11	9	2
1932	6	6	0	13	8	5

TABLE IV—1 (*continued*)

	Alcoholism deaths			Liver cirrhosis deaths		
	Total	Male	Female	Total	Male	Female
	J. Alberta (*continued*)					
1933	4	4	0	20	14	6
1934	4	4	0	15	10	5
1935	11	11	0	14	10	4
1936	12	12	0	20	15	5
1937	6	6	0	15	11	4
1938	7	7	0	17	10	7
1939	8	8	0	20	13	7
1940	10	8	2	17	11	6
1941	4	4	0	21	16	5
1942	0	0	0	21	8	13
1943	2	2	0	23	17	6
1944	1	1	0	23	13	10
1945	3	3	0	37	22	15
1946	6	5	1	25	18	7
1947	3	2	1	43	34	9
1948	5	4	1	35	25	10
1949	6	6	0	42	34	8
1950	—	—	—	28	17	11
1951	—	—	—	23	14	9
1952	—	—	—	27	16	11
1953	—	—	—	47	33	14
1954	—	—	—	41	31	10
1955	—	—	—	45	27	18
1956	—	—	—	40	27	13
	K. British Columbia					
1901	8	—	—	12	—	—
1902	8	—	—	17	—	—
1903	6	—	—	15	—	—
1904	12	—	—	13	—	—
1905	13	—	—	8	—	—
1906	14	—	—	7	—	—
1907	18	—	—	12	—	—
1908	15	—	—	10	—	—
1909	20	—	—	8	—	—
1910	28	—	—	19	—	—
1911	27	—	—	14	—	—
1912	55	—	—	9	—	—
1913	48	—	—	22	—	—
1914	32	—	—	20	—	—
1915	18	—	—	19	—	—
1916	18	—	—	15	—	—

TABLE IV—1 (*continued*)

	Alcoholism deaths			Liver cirrhosis deaths		
	Total	Male	Female	Total	Male	Female
K. British Columbia (*continued*)						
1917	18	—	—	15	—	—
1918*	2	—	—	9	—	—
1919	10	—	—	9	—	—
1920	9	—	—	16	—	—
1921	11	10	1	12	9	3
1922	15	15	0	18	14	4
1923	14	11	3	19	12	7
1924	27	24	3	25	21	4
1925	21	20	1	27	23	4
1926	23	17	6	18	11	7
1927	22	22	0	23	17	6
1928	27	25	2	28	21	7
1929	41	36	5	34	27	7
1930	31	27	4	19	15	4
1931	16	16	0	16	12	4
1932	16	13	3	27	19	8
1933	17	15	2	25	15	10
1934	9	8	1	21	16	5
1935	14	13	1	29	21	8
1936	18	16	2	30	21	9
1937	24	22	2	30	26	4
1938	24	20	4	45	32	13
1939	12	10	2	41	29	12
1940	15	13	2	41	24	17
1941	8	8	0	37	26	11
1942	10	10	0	58	39	19
1943	10	9	1	46	33	13
1944	4	4	0	47	31	16
1945	5	4	1	45	27	18
1946	10	7	3	73	50	23
1947	9	8	1	76	50	26
1948	11	9	2	87	55	32
1949	7	7	0	93	61	32
1950	—	—	—	48	33	15
1951	—	—	—	94	70	24
1952	—	—	—	93	56	37
1953	—	—	—	86	55	31
1954	—	—	—	85	49	36
1955	—	—	—	75	49	26
1956	—	—	—	113	72	41

*Figures for 1918 are for the period January 1 to June 30, inclusive.

TABLE IV—2

DEATHS FROM ALL CAUSES BY SEX IN CANADA AND PROVINCES, 1901–1956

(For sources and notes, see page 122.)

	Canada			Newfoundland		
	Total	Male	Female	Total	Male	Female
1921	101,155	—	—	—	—	—
1922	102,487	—	—	—	—	—
1923	105,330	—	—	—	—	—
1924	98,553	—	—	—	—	—
1925	98,777	—	—	—	—	—
1926	107,454	56,979	50,475	—	—	—
1927	105,292	56,265	49,027	—	—	—
1928	109,057	58,480	50,577	—	—	—
1929	113,515	60,920	52,595	—	—	—
1930	109,306	59,109	50,197	—	—	—
1931	104,517	56,529	47,988	—	—	—
1932	104,377	56,153	48,224	—	—	—
1933	101,968	54,725	47,243	—	—	—
1934	101,582	55,224	46,358	—	—	—
1935	105,567	57,206	48,361	—	—	—
1936	107,050	57,728	49,322	—	—	—
1937	113,824	62,109	51,715	—	—	—
1938	106,817	58,817	48,000	—	—	—
1939	108,951	59,907	49,044	—	—	—
1940	110,927	61,399	49,528	—	—	—
1941	114,639	63,852	50,787	—	—	—
1942	112,978	63,013	49,965	—	—	—
1943	118,635	66,013	52,622	—	—	—
1944	116,052	64,313	51,739	—	—	—
1945	113,414	63,351	50,063	—	—	—
1946	114,931	64,159	50,772	—	—	—
1947	117,704	66,438	51,266	—	—	—
1948	119,384	67,427	51,957	—	—	—
1949	121,179	68,775	52,404	2,868	1,596	1,272
1950	123,789	70,340	53,449	3,168	1,774	1,394
1951	125,454	71,353	54,101	3,004	1,615	1,389
1952	125,950	72,720	53,230	2,773	1,501	1,272
1953	127,381	73,417	53,964	2,733	1,544	1,189
1954	124,520	72,140	52,380	2,916	1,696	1,220
1955	128,154	74,701	53,453	3,206	1,804	1,402
1956	131,585	76,339	55,246	3,058	1,677	1,381

	Prince Edward Island			Nova Scotia		
1909	—	—	—	6,978	—	—
1910	—	—	—	7,120	—	—
1911	—	—	—	8,237	—	—
1912	—	—	—	7,126	—	—

TABLE IV—2 (continued)

	Prince Edward Island			Nova Scotia		
	Total	Male	Female	Total	Male	Female
1913	—	—	—	7,225	—	—
1914	—	—	—	7,527	—	—
1915	—	—	—	7,675	—	—
1916	—	—	—	8,052	—	—
1917	—	—	—	7,583	—	—
1918	—	—	—	9,125	—	—
1919	—	—	—	9,200	—	—
1920	—	—	—	7,439	—	—
1921	1,209	619	590	6,420	3,372	3,048
1922	1,113	588	525	6,679	3,515	3,164
1923	1,150	552	598	6,868	3,587	3,281
1924	956	490	466	6,583	3,456	3,127
1925	997	513	484	6,045	3,076	2,969
1926	898	452	446	6,366	3,370	2,992
1927	913	451	462	6,378	3,300	3,078
1928	952	495	457	6,202	3,339	2,863
1929	1,122	595	527	6,660	3,516	3,144
1930	961	511	450	6,206	3,279	2,927
1931	912	481	431	5,968	3,095	2,873
1932	1,051	543	508	6,159	3,232	2,927
1933	1,032	555	477	6,045	3,157	2,888
1934	1,033	517	516	6,028	3,179	2,849
1935	975	531	444	6,164	3,267	2,897
1936	1,024	534	490	5,897	3,157	2,740
1937	1,146	604	542	6,083	3,244	2,839
1938	1,030	551	479	6,087	3,264	2,823
1939	1,133	578	555	6,324	3,387	2,937
1940	1,067	575	492	6,239	3,399	2,840
1941	1,134	595	539	6,914	3,739	3,175
1942	961	503	458	6,385	3,503	2,882
1943	912	503	409	6,477	3,581	2,896
1944	926	488	438	6,229	3,362	2,867
1945	888	455	433	5,625	3,090	2,535
1946	874	476	398	6,046	3,266	2,780
1947	1,020	543	477	6,009	3,287	2,722
1948	887	455	432	6,097	3,331	2,766
1949	924	531	393	5,980	3,321	2,659
1950	903	464	439	6,078	3,396	2,682
1951	904	501	403	5,812	3,246	2,566
1952	916	503	413	5,756	3,253	2,503
1953	926	515	411	5,808	3,214	2,594
1954	966	531	435	5,692	3,222	2,470
1955	901	506	395	5,940	3,371	2,569
1956	933	548	385	5,738	3,251	2,487

TABLE IV—2 (*continued*)

	New Brunswick			Quebec		
	Total	Male	Female	Total	Male	Female
1901	—	—	—	30,582	—	—
1902	—	—	—	27,408	—	—
1903	—	—	—	30,876	—	—
1904	—	—	—	30,549	—	—
1905	—	—	—	29,071	—	—
1906	—	—	—	29,969	—	—
1907	—	—	—	29,007	—	—
1908	—	—	—	35,052	—	—
1909	—	—	—	33,231	—	—
1910	—	—	—	35,183	—	—
1911	—	—	—	35,904	—	—
1912	—	—	—	32,980	—	—
1913	—	—	—	36,200	—	—
1914	—	—	—	36,002	—	—
1915	—	—	—	35,933	—	—
1916	—	—	—	38,206	—	—
1917	—	—	—	35,501	—	—
1918	—	—	—	48,902	—	—
1919	—	—	—	35,170	—	—
1920	—	—	—	40,686	—	—
1921	5,410	2,858	2,552	33,433	—	—
1922	5,158	2,689	2,469	33,459	—	—
1923	5,013	2,618	2,395	35,148	—	—
1924	4,923	2,629	2,294	32,356	—	—
1925	4,960	2,620	2,340	32,300	—	—
1926	5,002	2,608	2,394	37,251	19,232	18,019
1927	4,902	2,537	2,365	36,175	18,827	17,348
1928	4,972	2,654	2,318	36,632	19,036	17,596
1929	5,230	2,718	2,512	37,221	19,235	17,986
1930	4,991	2,617	2,374	35,945	18,824	17,121
1931	4,644	2,449	2,195	34,487	18,067	16,420
1932	4,554	2,420	2,134	33,088	17,274	15,814
1933	4,908	2,601	2,307	31,636	16,455	15,181
1934	4,665	2,517	2,148	31,929	16,802	15,127
1935	4,779	2,559	2,220	32,839	17,160	15,679
1936	4,803	2,568	2,235	31,853	16,456	15,397
1937	5,433	2,885	2,548	35,456	18,694	16,762
1938	4,898	2,628	2,270	32,609	17,376	15,233
1939	5,082	2,781	2,301	33,388	17,545	15,843
1940	4,985	2,644	2,341	32,799	17,497	15,302
1941	5,184	2,804	2,380	34,338	18,344	15,994
1942	5,154	2,741	2,413	33,799	18,233	15,566
1943	4,917	2,677	2,240	35,069	18,915	16,154
1944	5,131	2,772	2,359	34,813	18,569	16,244
1945	4,865	2,635	2,230	33,348	18,002	15,346

TABLE IV—2 (*continued*)

	New Brunswick			Quebec		
	Total	Male	Female	Total	Male	Female
1946	4,866	2,611	2,255	33,690	18,062	15,628
1947	4,832	2,696	2,136	33,708	18,566	15,142
1948	4,959	2,668	2,291	33,603	18,358	15,245
1949	4,876	2,672	2,204	34,107	18,708	15,399
1950	4,895	2,690	2,205	33,507	18,396	15,111
1951	4,873	2,668	2,205	34,900	19,199	15,701
1952	4,647	2,661	1,986	34,854	19,710	14,144
1953	4,637	2,525	2,112	34,469	19,474	14,995
1954	4,286	2,463	1,823	33,169	18,668	14,501
1955	4,435	2,565	1,870	33,952	19,212	14,740
1956	4,658	2,580	2,078	35,042	19,796	15,246

	Ontario			Manitoba		
1901	28,500	—	—	—	—	—
1902	26,713	—	—	—	—	—
1903	28,399	—	—	—	—	—
1904	29,600	—	—	—	—	—
1905	29,746	—	—	—	—	—
1906	31,244	—	—	—	—	—
1907	31,756	—	—	—	—	—
1908	30,947	—	—	—	—	—
1909	30,792	—	—	—	—	—
1910	31,332	—	—	—	—	—
1911	31,878	—	—	—	—	—
1912	32,150	—	—	—	—	—
1913	34,317	—	—	—	—	—
1914	32,440	—	—	—	—	—
1915	33,294	—	—	—	—	—
1916	35,580	—	—	—	—	—
1917	33,284	—	—	—	—	—
1918	43,038	—	—	—	—	—
1919	34,010	—	—	—	—	—
1920	40,440	—	—	—	—	—
1921	34,551	13,062	16,489	5,388	2,964	2,424
1922	34,034	17,726	16,308	5,754	3,079	2,675
1923	35,636	18,452	17,184	5,330	2,935	2,395
1924	33,078	17,153	15,925	5,023	2,713	2,310
1925	33,960	17,583	16,377	5,245	2,911	2,334
1926	35,909	18,721	17,188	5,335	2,936	2,399
1927	34,775	18,305	16,470	5,309	2,968	2,341
1928	37,128	19,457	17,671	5,396	3,029	2,367
1929	38,123	20,281	17,842	5,808	3,247	2,561
1930	37,313	19,827	17,486	5,685	3,191	2,494
1931	35,705	19,137	16,568	5,319	3,016	2,303

TABLE IV—2 (*continued*)

	Ontario			Manitoba		
	Total	Male	Female	Total	Male	Female
1932	36,469	19,196	17,273	5,341	3,063	2,278
1933	35,301	18,489	16,812	5,455	3,092	2,363
1934	35,119	18,731	16,388	5,169	2,920	2,249
1935	36,317	19,281	17,036	5,781	3,246	2,535
1936	37,571	19,916	17,655	6,219	3,438	2,781
1937	38,475	20,690	17,785	6,070	3,441	2,629
1938	36,890	19,814	17,076	5,893	3,327	2,566
1939	37,530	20,310	17,220	6,157	3,531	2,626
1940	38,503	20,923	17,580	6,339	3,578	2,761
1941	39,226	21,549	17,677	6,495	3,782	2,713
1942	39,119	21,349	17,770	6,410	3,680	2,730
1943	41,063	22,159	18,904	7,007	4,009	2,998
1944	39,781	21,629	18,152	6,701	3,837	2,864
1945	39,499	21,563	17,936	6,550	3,775	2,775
1946	39,758	21,849	17,909	6,537	3,735	2,802
1947	41,619	22,891	18,728	6,750	3,924	2,826
1948	42,364	23,394	18,970	6,675	3,900	2,775
1949	43,379	24,123	19,256	6,919	4,008	2,911
1950	43,948	24,502	19,446	6,610	3,904	2,706
1951	43,981	24,483	19,498	6,735	3,986	2,749
1952	44,402	25,072	19,330	6,552	3,917	2,635
1953	45,242	25,347	19,895	7,015	4,224	2,791
1954	44,515	25,050	19,465	6,719	4,055	2,664
1955	45,434	25,890	19,544	6,853	4,080	2,773
1956	47,231	26,868	20,363	7,058	4,285	2,773

	Saskatchewan			Alberta			British Columbia		
	Total	Male	Female	Total	Male	Female	Total	Male	Female
1901	—	—	—	—	—	—	1,422	—	—
1902	—	—	—	—	—	—	1,607	—	—
1903	—	—	—	—	—	—	1,535	—	—
1904	—	—	—	—	—	—	1,687	—	—
1905	—	—	—	—	—	—	1,551	—	—
1906	—	—	—	—	—	—	1,739	—	—
1907	—	—	—	—	—	—	2,326	—	—
1908	—	—	—	—	—	—	2,445	—	—
1909	—	—	—	—	—	—	2,693	—	—
1910	—	—	—	—	—	—	3,115	—	—
1911	—	—	—	—	—	—	3,469	—	—
1912	—	—	—	—	—	—	4,073	—	—
1913	—	—	—	—	—	—	4,340	—	—
1914	—	—	—	—	—	—	3,739	—	—

TABLE IV—2 (*continued*)

	Saskatchewan			Alberta			British Columbia		
	Total	Male	Female	Total	Male	Female	Total	Male	Female
1915	—	—	—	—	—	—	3,586	—	—
1916	—	—	—	—	—	—	3,686	—	—
1917	—	—	—	—	—	—	3,721	—	—
1918	—	—	—	—	—	—	2,046*	—	—
1919	—	—	—	—	—	—	6,508	—	—
1920	—	—	—	—	—	—	4,618	—	—
1921	5,596	3,078	2,518	4,940	2,858	2,082	4,208	2,600	1,608
1922	6,119	3,411	2,708	5,264	2,984	2,280	4,907	3,052	1,855
1923	6,182	3,442	2,740	5,006	2,861	2,145	4,997	3,070	1,927
1924	5,772	3,176	2,596	4,858	2,718	2,140	5,004	3,080	1,924
1925	5,628	3,228	2,400	4,697	2,703	1,994	4,945	3,047	1,898
1926	6,060	3,393	2,667	5,159	2,931	2,288	5,474	3,332	2,142
1927	6,031	3,395	2,636	5,059	2,932	2,127	5,750	3,550	2,200
1928	6,166	3,485	2,681	5,699	3,322	2,377	5,910	2,663	2,247
1929	6,715	3,794	2,921	6,239	3,504	2,735	6,397	4,030	2,367
1930	6,309	3,670	2,639	5,496	3,171	2,325	6,400	4,019	2,381
1931	6,066	3,443	2,623	5,302	3,095	2,207	6,114	3,746	2,368
1932	6,044	3,469	2,575	5,521	3,248	2,273	6,150	3,708	2,442
1933	6,024	3,367	2,657	5,346	3,165	2,181	6,221	3,844	2,377
1934	5,924	3,423	2,501	5,337	3,149	2,188	6,378	3,986	2,392
1935	6,126	3,614	2,512	5,729	3,407	2,322	6,857	4,141	2,716
1936	6,314	3,616	2,698	6,147	3,610	2,537	7,222	4,433	2,789
1937	6,927	4,037	2,890	6,261	3,661	2,600	7,973	4,853	3,120
1938	6,079	3,673	2,406	5,871	3,481	2,390	7,460	4,703	2,757
1939	6,031	3,593	2,438	5,789	3,468	2,321	7,517	4,714	2,803
1940	6,477	3,852	2,625	6,203	3,683	2,520	8,315	5,248	3,067
1941	6,458	3,821	2,637	6,385	3,866	2,519	8,505	5,352	3,153
1942	6,190	3,665	2,525	6,091	3,724	2,367	8,869	5,615	3,254
1943	6,654	3,993	2,661	6,524	3,999	2,525	10,012	6,177	3,835
1944	6,454	3,830	2,624	6,320	3,823	2,497	9,697	6,003	3,694
1945	6,429	3,867	2,562	6,454	3,907	2,547	9,756	6,057	3,699
1946	6,422	3,866	2,556	6,601	4,049	2,552	10,137	6,245	3,892
1947	6,610	3,989	2,621	6,543	3,916	2,627	10,613	6,626	3,987
1948	6,496	4,012	2,484	6,987	4,254	2,733	11,316	7,055	4,261
1949	6,596	3,962	2,634	7,083	4,350	2,733	11,315	7,100	4,215
1950	6,243	3,821	2,422	6,856	4,189	2,667	11,581	7,204	4,377
1951	6,440	3,915	2,525	7,167	4,429	2,738	11,638	7,311	4,327
1952	6,625	4,100	2,525	7,345	4,561	2,784	12,080	7,442	4,638
1953	6,687	4,110	2,577	7,646	4,786	2,860	12,218	7,678	4,540
1954	6,323	4,001	2,322	7,520	4,778	2,742	12,414	7,676	4,738
1955	6,661	4,092	2,569	7,956	5,113	2,843	12,816	8,068	4,748
1956	6,666	4,158	2,508	7,786	4,916	2,870	13,415	8,260	5,155

*Figures for 1918 are for the period January 1 to June 30, inclusive.

97

TABLE IV—3

DEATHS ATTRIBUTED TO ALCOHOLISM, AND TO CIRRHOSIS OF THE LIVER PER 100,000
POPULATION AGED 20 AND OLDER, DEATHS FROM ALL CAUSES PER 100,000 POPULA-
TION OF ALL AGES, AND DEATHS FROM LIVER CIRRHOSIS PER 1,000 DEATHS FROM
ALL CAUSES IN CANADA AND PROVINCES, 1901–1956
(For sources and notes, see page 122.)

	Rate of death from alcoholism	Rate of death from liver cirrhosis	Rate of death from all causes	Liver cirrhosis deaths per 1,000 deaths from all causes
		A. Canada		
1901	2.1	8.8	1,751	2.7
1902	2.3	8.6	1,552	3.0
1903	2.8	11.4	1,680	3.6
1904	3.6	10.1	1,617	3.3
1905	3.2	10.4	1,505	3.7
1906	4.2	9.9	1,537	3.5
1907	5.0	9.3	1,394	3.8
1908	5.0	7.5	1,474	2.9
1909	5.1	8.6	1,415	3.5
1910	4.7	8.5	1,447	3.4
1911	5.8	9.0	1,467	3.5
1912	8.2	9.3	1,384	3.9
1913	7.5	10.1	1,449	4.0
1914	5.3	9.4	1,373	4.0
1915	4.1	8.4	1,377	3.5
1916	4.2	9.6	1,467	3.8
1917	3.9	8.3	1,367	3.5
1918	3.3	8.0	1,859	2.5
1919	2.7	6.5	1,379	2.7
1920	3.2	7.1	1,501	2.7
1921	2.3	5.9	1,153	2.9
1922	2.0	5.6	1,151	2.8
1923	2.7	6.5	1,171	3.1
1924	2.8	5.4	1,079	2.8
1925	2.8	7.3	1,064	3.9
1926	3.9	5.2	1,138	2.6
1927	4.1	6.3	1,094	3.3
1928	3.9	6.4	1,110	3.3
1929	4.3	6.3	1,133	3.2
1930	3.1	5.6	1,072	3.0
1931	2.4	6.1	1,009	3.5
1932	2.2	6.4	994	3.8
1933	1.6	5.8	960	3.6
1934	1.9	6.1	947	3.9
1935	2.4	6.4	975	3.9

TABLE IV—3 (*continued*)

	Rate of death from alcoholism	Rate of death from liver cirrhosis	Rate of death from all causes	Liver cirrhosis deaths per 1,000 deaths from all causes
A. Canada (*continued*)				
1936	2.8	6.8	979	4.2
1937	3.0	6.0	1,032	3.6
1938	2.4	7.1	959	4.5
1939	1.8	7.2	968	4.6
1940	2.1	6.5	976	4.1
1941	1.2	6.6	998	4.1
1942	0.8	7.7	971	5.0
1943	0.8	7.0	1,007	4.4
1944	0.9	6.6	973	4.3
1945	1.0	7.3	941	4.9
1946	1.2	7.7	937	5.2
1947	1.1	7.9	940	5.3
1948	1.0	8.1	934	5.5
1949	0.9	9.1	903	6.3
1950	—	7.2	904	5.0
1951	—	7.0	897	4.8
1952	—	7.3	874	5.2
1953	—	8.0	863	5.7
1954	—	8.0	821	6.0
1955	—	8.0	823	5.9
1956	—	8.8	828	6.4
B. Newfoundland				
1949	—	2.1	831	1.4
1950	—	1.6	903	0.9
1951	—	1.1	832	0.7
1952	—	2.0	741	1.4
1953	—	4.0	714	2.9
1954	—	2.4	733	1.7
1955	—	5.2	778	3.4
1956	—	2.3	721	1.6
C. Prince Edward Island				
1921	2.0	5.9	1,358	2.5
1922	0	1.9	1,251	0.9
1923	4.0	2.0	1,322	0.9
1924	2.0	2.0	1,112	1.0
1925	0	12.0	1,159	6.0
1926	6.0	2.0	1,032	1.1
1927	0	2.0	1,049	1.1

TABLE IV—3 (*continued*)

	Rate of death from alcoholism	Rate of death from liver cirrhosis	Rate of death from all causes	Liver cirrhosis deaths per 1,000 deaths from all causes
C. Prince Edward Island (*continued*)				
1928	0	0	1,082	0
1929	2.0	5.9	1,275	2.7
1930	3.9	3.9	1,092	2.1
1931	0	0	1,036	0
1932	0	5.8	1,181	2.9
1933	0	3.8	1,147	1.9
1934	1.9	5.6	1,135	2.9
1935	1.8	3.6	1,060	2.1
1936	5.3	1.8	1,101	1.0
1937	7.1	5.4	1,232	2.6
1938	0	0	1,096	0
1939	3.5	7.0	1,205	3.5
1940	3.4	0	1,123	0
1941	0	7.0	1,194	3.5
1942	0	5.6	1,068	3.1
1943	0	9.1	1,002	5.5
1944	5.5	3.6	1,018	2.2
1945	1.8	7.1	965	4.5
1946	1.8	8.8	930	5.7
1947	1.8	3.5	1,085	2.0
1948	1.8	0	954	0
1949	0	10.9	983	6.5
1950	—	7.1	941	4.4
1951	—	7.0	922	4.4
1952	—	3.3	889	2.2
1953	—	0	874	0
1954	—	6.6	920	4.1
1955	—	6.3	834	4.4
1956	—	5.0	889	3.2
D. Nova Scotia				
1909	4.1	8.9	1,445	3.4
1910	2.6	5.5	1,465	2.1
1911	1.8	3.6	1,674	1.2
1912	2.9	8.9	1,437	3.5
1913	5.3	6.4	1,434	2.5
1914	4.9	7.0	1,470	2.7
1915	3.1	7.7	1,502	2.9
1916	—	—	1,594	—
1917	3.2	2.1	1,508	0.8
1918	1.4	6.4	1,818	2.0

TABLE IV—3 (*continued*)

	Rate of death from alcoholism	Rate of death from liver cirrhosis	Rate of death from all causes	Liver cirrhosis deaths per 1,000 deaths from all causes
D. Nova Scotia (*continued*)				
1919	2.5	2.5	1,815	0.8
1920	2.4	3.8	1,442	1.5
1921	2.0	3.7	1,225	1.7
1922	2.7	4.4	1,280	1.9
1923	1.4	4.5	1,326	1.9
1924	2.1	3.1	1,276	1.4
1925	3.8	4.1	1,174	2.0
1926	2.1	5.1	1,236	2.4
1927	2.7	5.1	1,238	2.4
1928	6.1	3.1	1,204	1.5
1929	2.7	4.4	1,293	2.0
1930	5.1	4.1	1,207	1.9
1931	5.1	5.5	1,163	2.7
1932	1.7	4.4	1,187	2.1
1933	1.0	4.6	1,151	2.3
1934	4.2	6.8	1,135	3.5
1935	4.1	3.8	1,150	1.9
1936	2.5	5.2	1,086	2.9
1937	3.6	2.4	1,108	1.3
1938	1.2	3.9	1,097	2.1
1939	1.8	5.9	1,127	3.2
1940	1.8	5.5	1,096	3.0
1941	2.3	3.7	1,196	1.9
1942	0.8	5.2	1,080	3.0
1943	1.3	4.3	1,069	2.5
1944	0.5	3.4	1,019	2.1
1945	1.3	5.8	909	3.9
1946	2.4	3.7	994	2.3
1947	1.6	4.5	977	2.8
1948	1.8	6.9	976	4.3
1949	0.8	5.3	951	3.3
1950	—	4.2	953	2.6
1951	—	4.2	904	2.8
1952	—	6.2	881	4.2
1953	—	6.6	876	4.5
1954	—	7.6	846	5.3
1955	—	6.0	870	4.0
1956	—	5.7	824	4.0
E. New Brunswick				
1921	1.4	6.2	1,394	2.4
1922	1.0	2.4	1,326	1.0

TABLE IV—3 (*continued*)

	Rate of death from alcoholism	Rate of death from liver cirrhosis	Rate of death from all causes	Liver cirrhosis deaths per 1,000 deaths from all causes
		E. New Brunswick (*continued*)		
1923	4.3	4.8	1,289	2.0
1924	2.4	1.9	1,259	0.8
1925	3.7	6.6	1,262	2.8
1926	1.9	5.1	1,263	2.2
1927	4.2	5.1	1,232	2.2
1928	0.9	4.1	1,240	1.8
1929	8.2	3.7	1,295	1.5
1930	1.8	5.9	1,229	2.6
1931	3.2	3.2	1,138	1.5
1932	2.2	4.5	1,100	2.2
1933	2.6	3.9	1,171	1.8
1934	3.4	3.0	1,103	1.5
1935	2.9	5.0	1,117	2.5
1936	7.0	4.9	1,109	2.5
1937	4.5	2.4	1,243	1.1
1938	3.6	5.6	1,108	2.9
1939	1.2	7.1	1,137	3.5
1940	4.6	5.0	1,103	2.6
1941	1.5	2.7	1,134	1.4
1942	0.4	4.1	1,111	2.1
1943	1.1	5.2	1,062	2.8
1944	1.9	1.9	1,113	1.0
1945	2.2	3.7	1,042	2.1
1946	2.5	3.8	1,018	2.3
1947	2.1	5.0	900	2.9
1948	2.4	4.5	996	2.6
1949	3.4	7.6	960	4.5
1950	—	5.2	956	3.1
1951	—	3.1	944	1.8
1952	—	6.8	883	4.3
1953	—	4.7	865	3.0
1954	—	5.9	784	4.2
1955	—	4.5	795	3.2
1956	—	6.4	819	4.2
		F. Quebec		
1901	2.4	8.7	1,855	2.4
1902	2.5	8.0	1,641	2.5
1903	4.1	11.6	1,807	3.3
1904	5.3	10.5	1,744	3.1
1905	3.0	11.6	1,642	3.6
1906	5.1	11.3	1,680	3.4

TABLE IV—3 (*continued*)

	Rate of death from alcoholism	Rate of death from liver cirrhosis	Rate of death from all causes	Liver cirrhosis deaths per 1,000 deaths from all causes
		F. Quebec (*continued*)		
1907	5.8	14.1	1,565	4.6
1908	4.9	9.8	1,843	2.7
1909	3.9	12.8	1,721	3.8
1910	3.8	12.0	1,790	3.4
1911	5.0	13.0	1,790	3.7
1912	4.7	15.1	1,615	4.8
1913	5.8	15.6	1,727	4.6
1914	4.0	14.6	1,676	4.5
1915	3.9	12.8	1,662	4.0
1916	5.0	14.5	1,774	4.2
1917	4.4	13.7	1,637	4.3
1918	5.2	14.7	2,232	3.4
1919	3.0	11.6	1,574	3.8
1920	3.0	11.2	1,770	3.3
1921	2.8	12.1	1,416	4.4
1922	0.5	9.8	1,389	3.7
1923	1.0	12.0	1,437	4.4
1924	1.7	8.7	1,297	3.5
1925	1.5	12.7	1,267	5.3
1926	3.8	9.1	1,431	3.4
1927	4.0	9.4	1,361	3.6
1928	3.2	11.6	1,349	4.6
1929	2.2	11.3	1,343	4.5
1930	2.2	10.5	1,272	4.4
1931	2.3	11.7	1,200	5.3
1932	1.6	11.7	1,131	5.7
1933	0.8	9.4	1,064	4.9
1934	1.4	10.7	1,059	5.6
1935	2.7	10.9	1,074	5.6
1936	5.0	12.3	1,028	6.6
1937	3.7	10.4	1,129	5.1
1938	2.5	10.8	1,024	5.9
1939	2.1	10.4	1,034	5.7
1940	2.7	9.7	1,001	5.5
1941	0.9	10.0	1,031	5.6
1942	0.7	11.5	997	6.7
1943	0.6	10.9	1,030	6.3
1944	1.0	10.1	995	5.9
1945	0.4	10.7	937	6.7
1946	0.8	10.8	928	6.8
1947	1.0	9.8	909	6.3
1948	0.7	9.1	887	6.0

TABLE IV—3 (*continued*)

	Rate of death from alcoholism	Rate of death from liver cirrhosis	Rate of death from all causes	Liver cirrhosis deaths per 1,000 deaths from all causes
F. Quebec (*continued*)				
1949	0.9	10.8	879	7.2
1950	—	8.7	844	6.0
1951	—	8.2	860	5.6
1952	—	7.8	835	5.4
1953	—	8.5	807	6.1
1954	—	8.0	756	6.2
1955	—	9.1	751	6.9
1956	—	9.7	756	7.3
G. Ontario				
1901	1.4	—	—	—
1902	1.9	—	—	—
1903	1.8	—	—	—
1904	2.1	—	—	—
1905	2.8	—	—	—
1906	3.1	—	—	—
1907	3.8	6.6	1,343	2.9
1908	4.9	6.3	1,283	3.0
1909	5.6	7.6	1,260	3.2
1910	4.6	6.9	1,262	3.3
1911	6.3	7.9	1,261	3.8
1912	9.5	6.6	1,250	3.2
1913	7.3	7.5	1,300	3.5
1914	5.4	7.0	1,199	3.5
1915	4.0	6.0	1,222	3.0
1916	3.3	7.2	1,311	3.4
1917	3.3	6.3	1,222	3.2
1918	2.4	3.8	1,568	1.5
1919	2.3	4.0	1,219	2.0
1920	3.6	5.3	1,413	2.3
1921	2.2	4.5	1,178	2.3
1922	2.2	5.0	1,142	2.7
1923	3.3	5.3	1,183	2.8
1924	2.6	4.4	1,081	2.5
1925	2.9	5.8	1,091	3.3
1926	4.4	3.8	1,135	2.1
1927	4.1	6.2	1,080	3.6
1928	3.6	5.1	1,133	2.8
1929	4.5	5.4	1,143	2.9
1930	3.5	4.1	1,102	2.4
1931	2.4	5.0	1,040	3.0
1932	3.1	5.3	1,050	3.2

TABLE IV—3 (*continued*)

	Rate of death from alcoholism	Rate of death from liver cirrhosis	Rate of death from all causes	Liver cirrhosis deaths per 1,000 deaths from all causes
G. Ontario (*continued*)				
1933	2.1	4.9	1,005	3.1
1934	2.0	5.3	991	3.5
1935	2.5	5.0	1,016	3.2
1936	2.6	5.0	1,042	3.2
1937	2.6	5.4	1,058	3.4
1938	2.4	6.4	1,005	4.2
1939	1.8	6.4	1,012	4.2
1940	1.8	6.2	1,028	4.0
1941	1.1	5.8	1,036	3.7
1942	0.8	6.5	1,007	4.3
1943	0.8	5.7	1,049	3.7
1944	1.1	5.6	1,004	3.7
1945	1.2	6.0	987	4.1
1946	1.3	6.4	971	4.5
1947	1.1	7.8	997	5.3
1948	1.3	7.8	991	5.3
1949	0.8	8.9	991	6.0
1950	—	8.2	983	5.5
1951	—	7.1	957	4.9
1952	—	7.6	932	5.4
1953	—	8.4	924	6.0
1954	—	8.9	882	6.5
1955	—	8.8	877	6.4
1956	—	9.2	890	6.6
H. Manitoba				
1921	3.0	1.8	883	1.1
1922	0.9	2.4	934	1.4
1923	2.7	3.6	861	2.3
1924	4.1	4.4	804	3.0
1925	2.6	3.5	830	2.3
1926	4.3	3.7	835	2.4
1927	6.6	3.9	816	2.6
1928	5.1	4.6	813	3.2
1929	5.7	2.3	858	1.5
1930	1.5	3.0	825	2.1
1931	2.7	2.5	760	1.9
1932	1.9	3.4	758	2.6
1933	1.0	4.3	770	3.3
1934	1.9	4.7	729	3.9
1935	1.4	5.6	814	4.2
1936	2.8	5.1	875	3.5

TABLE IV—3 (*continued*)

	Rate of death from alcoholism	Rate of death from liver cirrhosis	Rate of death from all causes	Liver cirrhosis deaths per 1,000 deaths from all causes
H. Manitoba (*continued*)				
1937	2.7	3.2	849	2.3
1938	1.3	5.8	818	4.4
1939	1.3	5.9	848	4.4
1940	1.1	3.9	871	2.8
1941	1.7	7.1	890	5.1
1942	1.7	6.0	885	4.4
1943	0.4	5.8	969	3.9
1944	0.2	5.7	922	4.0
1945	1.9	5.9	901	4.3
1946	0.6	6.6	899	4.7
1947	0.8	3.3	913	2.4
1948	0	8.3	895	6.0
1949	0.6	6.3	914	4.5
1950	—	5.7	861	4.2
1951	—	5.2	867	3.9
1952	—	5.5	821	4.3
1953	—	6.8	867	5.0
1954	—	7.1	811	5.5
1955	—	6.4	807	5.0
1956	—	7.7	817	5.8
I. Saskatchewan				
1921	0.5	2.8	738	2.0
1922	2.8	3.3	796	2.1
1923	2.7	3.7	795	2.4
1924	2.0	2.9	635	2.1
1925	3.1	5.0	698	3.7
1926	1.9	3.8	738	2.6
1927	3.4	2.3	717	2.3
1928	3.0	3.1	715	1.7
1929	3.0	1.7	760	1.2
1930	3.1	3.3	699	2.5
1931	1.6	3.6	658	3.0
1932	0.6	2.4	654	2.0
1933	0.6	2.6	651	2.2
1934	1.3	1.2	638	1.0
1935	0.6	4.2	659	3.6
1936	0.4	4.2	678	3.5
1937	1.3	3.6	751	2.7
1938	1.9	4.2	665	3.6
1939	0.6	4.4	666	3.8

TABLE IV—3 (*continued*)

	Rate of death from alcoholism	Rate of death from liver cirrhosis	Rate of death from all causes	Liver cirrhosis deaths per 1,000 deaths from all causes
I. Saskatchewan (*continued*)				
1940	1.3	3.2	720	2.6
1941	0.9	3.9	721	3.3
1942	0.4	5.5	730	4.5
1943	0.2	4.3	794	3.3
1944	0.2	5.9	772	4.6
1945	0.8	5.5	772	4.4
1946	0.4	5.9	771	4.7
1947	0.6	5.3	791	4.1
1948	0.2	5.8	775	4.6
1949	0	7.5	793	5.8
1950	—	5.9	749	4.8
1951	—	4.3	774	3.4
1952	—	5.1	786	3.9
1953	—	5.5	777	4.3
1954	—	5.5	720	4.6
1955	—	4.3	749	3.5
1956	—	4.6	743	3.8
J. Alberta				
1921	2.8	2.5	839	1.6
1922	3.7	3.1	889	1.9
1923	4.0	2.7	844	1.8
1924	4.6	4.6	814	3.1
1925	3.0	3.0	780	2.1
1926	3.3	2.7	849	1.7
1927	3.1	4.6	799	3.2
1928	5.7	3.8	866	2.5
1929	4.7	3.1	912	1.9
1930	1.5	3.0	776	2.2
1931	2.9	2.6	724	2.1
1932	1.4	3.1	746	2.4
1933	0.9	4.6	713	3.7
1934	0.9	3.4	704	2.8
1935	2.4	3.1	749	2.4
1936	2.6	4.4	795	3.3
1937	1.3	3.2	807	2.4
1938	1.5	3.6	752	2.9
1939	1.7	4.2	737	3.5
1940	2.0	3.5	785	2.7
1941	0.8	4.3	802	3.3
1942	0	4.4	785	3.4

TABLE IV—3 (*continued*)

	Rate of death from alcoholism	Rate of death from liver cirrhosis	Rate of death from all causes	Liver cirrhosis deaths per 1,000 deaths from all causes
		J. Alberta (*continued*)		
1943	0.4	4.7	831	3.5
1944	0.2	4.5	782	3.6
1945	0.8	7.3	799	5.7
1946	1.2	5.0	822	3.8
1947	0.6	8.4	793	6.6
1948	0.9	6.6	818	5.0
1949	1.1	7.7	800	5.9
1950	—	5.0	751	4.1
1951	—	4.0	762	3.2
1952	—	4.5	757	3.7
1953	—	7.7	763	6.1
1954	—	6.5	724	5.5
1955	—	7.1	746	5.7
1956	—	6.2	713	5.1
		K. British Columbia		
1901	6.6	9.9	794	8.4
1902	5.9	12.6	808	10.6
1903	4.0	10.0	698	9.8
1904	7.3	7.9	697	7.7
1905	7.2	4.4	588	5.2
1906	7.3	3.6	623	4.0
1907	8.5	5.6	753	5.2
1908	6.6	4.3	741	4.1
1909	8.2	3.2	769	3.0
1910	10.9	7.4	842	6.1
1911	10.0	5.1	883	4.0
1912	20.0	3.1	1,001	2.2
1913	16.5	7.6	1,024	5.1
1914	10.6	6.6	846	5.3
1915	5.9	6.3	797	5.3
1916	5.9	4.9	808	4.1
1917	5.8	4.9	802	4.0
1918	—	—	—	—
1919	3.1	2.8	1,334	1.4
1920	2.7	4.9	911	3.5
1921	3.3	3.6	802	2.9
1922	4.3	5.1	907	3.7
1923	3.9	5.3	900	3.8
1924	7.3	6.7	876	5.0

TABLE IV—3 (*continued*)

	Rate of death from alcoholism	Rate of death from liver cirrhosis	Rate of death from all causes	Liver cirrhosis deaths per 1,000 deaths from all causes
		K. British Columbia (*continued*)		
1925	5.5	7.0	841	5.5
1926	5.8	4.5	903	3.3
1927	5.4	5.6	923	4.0
1928	6.4	6.6	922	4.7
1929	9.4	7.8	971	5.3
1930	6.9	4.2	947	3.0
1931	3.5	3.5	881	2.6
1932	3.4	5.7	870	4.4
1933	3.5	5.2	868	4.0
1934	1.8	4.2	877	3.3
1935	2.7	5.7	932	4.2
1936	3.4	5.7	969	4.2
1937	4.5	5.6	1,050	3.8
1938	4.4	8.3	963	6.0
1939	2.2	7.4	949	5.5
1940	2.6	7.2	1,033	4.9
1941	1.4	6.4	1,040	4.4
1942	1.6	9.5	1,019	6.5
1943	1.6	7.3	1,112	4.6
1944	0.6	7.2	1,040	4.8
1945	0.8	6.8	1,028	4.6
1946	1.4	10.4	1,011	7.2
1947	1.2	10.5	1,017	7.2
1948	1.5	11.6	1,046	7.7
1949	0.9	12.2	1,017	8.2
1950	—	6.2	1.019	4.1
1951	—	11.9	999	8.1
1952	—	11.6	1,008	7.7
1953	—	10.5	993	7.0
1954	—	10.2	981	6.8
1955	—	8.8	982	5.9
1956	—	13.0	992	8.4

TABLE IV—4

First Admissions and Readmissions for Alcoholism and for All Causes to Mental Institutions in Canada, 1939–1956

(For sources and notes, see page 122.)

	First admissions				Readmissions	
	Alcoholism with psychosis	Alcoholism without psychosis	Total alcoholism	All causes	Total alcoholism	All causes
1939	133	104	237	8,301	47	2,250
1940	126	41	167	7,736	26	2,087
1941	141	57	198	7,902	46	2,401
1942	154	44	198	8,410	36	2,282
1943	92	27	119	8,556	26	2,390
1944	113	37	150	9,170	31	2,629
1945	138	51	189	9,489	36	2,779
1946	187	95	282	9,752	46	3,144
1947	259	111	370	9,745	58	3,335
1948	250	148	398	10,685	57	3,499
1949	300	262	562	11,556	68	3,920
1950	274	269	543	11,912	251	4,499
1951	288	384	672	13,152	301	4,591
1952	324	450	774	15,056	397	5,901
1953	310	822	1,132	15,925	1,042	7,205
1954	377	1,082	1,459	20,627	1,456	8,724
1955	443	1,323	1,766	21,774	1,834	10,448
1956	579	1,475	2,054	19,802	1,954	10,133

TABLE IV—5

TRENDS IN ADMISSIONS FOR ALCOHOLISM TO MENTAL INSTITUTIONS IN CANADA, 1939–56

(For sources and notes, see page 123.)

	First admissions for alcoholism			Re-admissions	First admission rates	
	% with psychosis among all first alcoholism admissions	% without psychosis among all first alcoholism admissions	% total alcoholism among first admissions for all causes	% total alcoholism among re-admissions for all causes	Total alcoholism per 100,000 of 20 and older	All causes per 100,000 of all ages
1939	56.1	43.9	2.9	2.1	3.4	73.8
1940	75.4	24.6	2.2	1.2	2.4	68.1
1941	71.2	28.8	2.5	1.9	2.8	68.8
1942	77.8	22.2	2.4	1.6	2.7	72.3
1943	77.3	22.7	1.4	1.1	1.6	72.6
1944	75.3	24.7	1.6	1.2	2.0	76.9
1945	73.0	27.0	2.0	1.3	2.5	78.7
1946	66.3	33.7	2.9	1.5	3.6	79.5
1947	70.0	30.0	3.8	1.7	4.7	77.8
1948	62.8	37.2	3.7	1.6	4.9	83.6
1949	53.4	46.6	4.9	1.7	6.7	86.1
1950	50.5	49.5	4.6	5.6	6.4	87.0
1951	42.9	57.1	5.1	6.6	7.7	94.1
1952	41.9	58.1	5.1	6.7	8.7	104.5
1953	27.4	72.6	7.1	14.5	12.5	107.9
1954	25.8	74.2	7.1	16.7	15.7	136.0
1955	25.1	74.9	8.1	17.6	18.7	139.8
1956	28.2	71.8	10.4	19.3	21.4	124.2

TABLE IV—6

FIRST ADMISSIONS FOR ALCOHOLISM AND FOR ALL CAUSES TO MENTAL INSTITUTIONS IN EACH PROVINCE, 1950–1956
(For sources and notes, see page 123.)

	Alcoholism with psychosis	Alcoholism without psychosis	Total alcoholism	Total alcoholism per 100,000 of 20 and older	All causes	All causes per 100,000 of all ages	% total alcoholism among first admissions for all causes
A. Newfoundland							
1950	6	2	8	4.2	146	42	5.5
1951	4	29	33	17.3	175	48	18.9
1952	1	21	22	11.2	222	59	9.9
1953	1	12	13	6.5	267	70	4.9
1954	4	5	9	4.3	178	45	5.1
1955	1	0	1	0.5	143	35	0.6
1956	3	2	5	2.3	166	39	3.0
B. Prince Edward Island							
1950	0	14	14	25.0	41	42	34.1
1951	6	17	23	40.4	89	91	25.8
1952	4	17	21	35.0	104	101	20.2
1953	6	37	43	70.5	121	114	35.5
1954	2	24	26	52.6	114	109	22.8
1955	6	30	36	57.1	110	102	32.7
1956	3	30	33	55.0	146	139	22.6
C. Nova Scotia							
1950	45	0	45	11.8	538	84	8.4
1951	57	0	57	14.9	628	98	9.1
1952	49	13	62	16.1	674	103	9.2
1953	9	66	75	19.2	844	127	8.9
1954	9	61	70	17.7	1,166	173	6.0
1955	4	70	74	18.5	1,298	190	5.7
1956	10	110	120	29.6	828	119	14.4

TABLE IV—6 (continued)

	Alcoholism with psychosis	Alcoholism without psychosis	Total alcoholism	Total alcoholism per 100,000 of 20 and older	All causes	All causes per 100,000 of all ages	% total alcoholism among first admissions for all causes
D. New Brunswick							
1950	15	26	41	14.1	353	69	11.6
1951	3	36	39	13.5	354	69	11.0
1952	2	51	53	18.0	405	77	13.1
1953	10	52	62	20.8	405	76	15.3
1954	9	47	56	18.5	488	89	11.5
1955	5	81	86	27.9	752	135	11.4
1956	7	86	93	29.6	629	111	14.7
E. Quebec							
1950	47	12	59	2.6	2,589	65	2.3
1951	51	25	76	3.2	3,039	75	2.5
1952	79	15	94	3.9	4,495	108	2.1
1953	67	26	93	3.8	4,563	107	2.0
1954	123	287	410	16.1	4,843	110	8.5
1955	153	231	384	14.9	5,080	112	7.6
1956	233	222	455	17.3	4,184	90	10.9
F. Ontario							
1950	101	66	167	5.6	4,112	92	4.1
1951	84	81	165	5.4	4,395	96	3.8
1952	87	100	187	6.0	4,398	92	4.3
1953	118	174	292	9.1	4,837	99	6.0
1954	123	154	277	8.5	6,796	135	4.1
1955	154	411	565	17.0	7,203	139	7.8
1956	195	429	624	18.6	7,579	143	8.2

TABLE IV-6 (*continued*)

	Alcoholism with psychosis	Alcoholism without psychosis	Total alcoholism	Total alcoholism per 100,000 of 20 and older	All causes	All causes per 100,000 of all ages	% total alcoholism among first admissions for all causes
G. Manitoba							
1950	12	21	33	6.7	610	79	5.4
1951	16	22	38	7.6	586	75	6.5
1952	17	27	44	8.7	581	73	7.6
1953	10	32	42	8.2	528	65	8.0
1954	12	21	33	6.3	1,152	139	2.9
1955	17	55	72	13.6	981	116	7.3
1956	23	75	98	18.4	1,027	119	9.5
H. Saskatchewan							
1950	5	27	32	6.3	1,000	120	3.2
1951	11	25	36	7.1	1,029	124	3.5
1952	10	50	60	11.7	1,117	133	5.4
1953	12	70	82	15.6	1,119	130	7.3
1954	1	72	73	13.7	1,134	129	6.4
1955	6	64	70	13.1	1,173	132	6.0
1956	8	63	71	13.1	1,375	153	5.2

TABLE IV—6 (continued)

	Alcoholism with psychosis	Alcoholism without psychosis	Total alcoholism	Total alcoholism per 100,000 of 20 and older	All causes	All causes per 100,000 of all ages	% total alcoholism among first admissions for all causes
I. Alberta							
1950	16	24	40	7.1	669	73	6.0
1951	13	20	33	5.7	644	69	5.1
1952	33	26	59	9.9	737	76	8.0
1953	29	66	95	15.6	952	95	10.0
1954	35	69	104	16.6	1,611	155	6.5
1955	39	60	99	15.6	1,770	166	5.6
1956	34	85	119	18.4	1,321	121	9.0
J. British Columbia							
1950	27	77	104	13.3	1,854	163	5.6
1951	43	129	172	21.7	2,213	190	7.8
1952	42	130	172	21.4	2,323	194	7.4
1953	48	287	335	41.0	2,289	186	14.6
1954	59	342	401	48.2	3,154	249	12.7
1955	58	321	379	44.7	3,264	250	11.6
1956	63	373	436	50.3	2,547	188	17.1

TABLE IV—7

ESTIMATES OF THE TOTAL NUMBER OF ALCOHOLICS AND OF THE RATE OF ALCOHOLISM
IN CANADA AND PROVINCES, 1935–1956

(For sources and notes, see page 123.)

	Canada		Newfoundland		Prince Edward Island	
	Total alcoholics	Alcoholics per 100,000 (20 years and older)	Total alcoholics	Alcoholics per 100,000 (20 years and older)	Total alcoholics	Alcoholics per 100,000 (20 years and older)
1935	72,580	1,110	—	—	350	640
1936	74,660	1,130	—	—	300	530
1937	75,480	1,120	—	—	300	535
1938	80,880	1,180	—	—	300	530
1939	84,000	1,210	—	—	350	610
1940	81,880	1,160	—	—	350	600
1941	85,210	1,190	—	—	480	840
1942	91,820	1,255	—	—	650	1,200
1943	91,340	1,230	—	—	650	1,180
1944	90,180	1,190	—	—	560	1,020
1945	95,710	1,250	—	—	650	1,160
1946	102,800	1,320	—	—	690	1,210
1947	108,420	1,370	—	—	390	680
1948	116,590	1,445	—	—	350	640
1949	126,470	1,540	—	—	730	1,330
1950	130,790	1,530	600	315	900	1,610
1951	132,260	1,520	590	310	750	1,315
1952	140,580	1,580	960	490	430	720
1953	151,720	1,670	1,330	670	320	520
1954	158,120	1,700	1,560	760	640	1,050
1955	164,835	1,750	1,710	810	800	1,270
1956	180,990	1,890	1,865	860	750	1,250

	Nova Scotia		New Brunswick	
	Total alcoholics	Alcoholics per 100,000 (20 and older)	Total alcoholics	Alcoholics per 100,000 (20 and older)
1935	2,680	845	1,860	780
1936	2,330	720	1,815	740
1937	1,990	600	1,640	660
1938	2,330	695	2,250	900
1939	3,110	910	2,720	1,070
1940	3,070	880	2,205	850
1941	2,770	780	1,640	620
1942	2,900	800	1,860	690
1943	2,770	740	1,900	710
1944	2,770	730	1,470	550
1945	3,070	805	1,560	570

TABLE IV—7 (*continued*)

	Nova Scotia		New Brunswick	
	Total alcoholics	Alcoholics per 100,000 (20 and older)	Total alcoholics	Alcoholics per 100,000 (20 and older)
1946	2,900	775	1,990	715
1947	3,200	850	2,250	800
1948	3,850	1,015	2,680	940
1949	3,710	980	3,265	1,125
1950	3,420	890	3,030	1,040
1951	3,840	1,005	2,825	980
1952	4,800	1,240	3,360	1,140
1953	5,650	1,445	3,520	1,180
1954	5,860	1,480	3,410	1,125
1955	5,380	1,345	3,520	1,140
1956	4,690	1,160	3,890	1,240

	Quebec		Ontario	
1935	32,725	1,940	20,530	890
1936	33,935	1,990	20,920	890
1937	33,030	1,890	22,955	960
1938	32,680	1,830	25,635	1,060
1939	32,640	1,780	26,800	1,095
1940	32,210	1,720	26,370	1,060
1941	34,150	1,780	26,630	1,055
1942	37,260	1,900	27,540	1,060
1943	37,700	1,870	26,800	1,020
1944	37,005	1,810	26,330	990
1945	38,090	1,830	28,060	1,040
1946	38,690	1,820	31,820	1,150
1947	37,050	1,705	36,360	1,290
1948	37,180	1,680	40,120	1,400
1949	40,550	1,790	45,130	1,545
1950	42,245	1,830	48,700	1,635
1951	41,420	1,760	48,830	1,600
1952	41,740	1,720	51,440	1,640
1953	43,450	1,760	56,935	1,780
1954	45,470	1,790	60,770	1,860
1955	49,420	1,910	63,070	1,900
1956	56,615	2,150	68,930	2,050

	Manitoba		Saskatchewan	
1935	3,890	910	3,110	600
1936	3,545	820	3,675	700
1937	3,285	740	3,545	670
1938	4,020	895	3,720	710

117

TABLE IV—7 (*continued*)

	Manitoba		Saskatchewan	
	Total alcoholics	Alcoholics per 100,000 (20 and older)	Total alcoholics	Alcoholics per 100,000 (20 and older)
1939	4,240	930	3,675	700
1940	4,150	900	3,370	640
1941	4,840	1,040	3,760	710
1942	5,015	1,080	4,280	840
1943	4,710	1,000	4,410	870
1944	4,710	990	4,755	930
1945	4,930	1,040	5,010	980
1946	4,580	970	4,970	970
1947	4,450	925	4,930	960
1948	5,490	1,140	5,400	1,055
1949	5,900	1,210	6,180	1,210
1950	5,710	1,155	6,010	1,180
5951	5,760	1,160	5,330	1,050
1952	6,240	1,230	5,490	1,070
1953	7,200	1,410	6,020	1,150
1954	7,620	1,460	5,860	1,100
1955	7,780	1,470	5,330	990
1956	8,370	1,570	5,280	975
	Alberta		British Columbia	
1935	2,720	600	4,710	925
1936	2,980	650	5,140	980
1937	2,900	620	5,840	1,100
1938	2,980	630	6,960	1,280
1939	3,200	670	7,260	1,305
1940	3,240	670	6,920	1,220
1941	3,460	710	7,480	1,300
1942	3,720	775	8,600	1,400
1943	3,890	795	8,520	1,345
1944	4,580	905	8,000	1,225
1945	5,270	1,040	9,080	1,370
1946	5,620	1,120	11,540	1,650
1947	6,310	1,230	13,500	1,860
1948	6,700	1,270	14,830	1,980
1949	6,640	1,210	14,360	1,880
1950	6,030	1,070	14,140	1,820
1951	5,380	930	17,540	2,220
1952	6,610	1,110	19,510	2,420
1953	8,640	1,420	18,660	2,280
1954	9,280	1,480	17,650	2,120
1955	9,120	1,430	18,550	2,190
1956	8,960	1,390	21,640	2,495

TABLE IV—8

RATE OF REPORTED DEATH FROM ALCOHOLISM, LIVER CIRRHOSIS, AND FROM ALL CAUSES; RATE OF FIRST MENTAL INSTITUTION ADMISSION FOR ALCOHOLISM WITH AND WITHOUT PSYCHOSIS; AND THE ESTIMATED PREVALENCE OF ALCOHOLISM IN CANADA AND PROVINCES*

(For sources and notes, see page 123.)

	Alcoholism deaths per 100,000 (20 and older) (1949)	Liver cirrhosis deaths per 100,000 (20 and older) (1956)	Deaths from all causes per 100,000 (all ages) (1956)	Admissions for alcoholism per 100,000 (20 and older) (1956)	Alcoholics per 100,000 (20 and older) (1956)
Canada	0.9	8.8	828	18.7	1,890
Newfoundland	—	2.3	721	2.3	860
Prince Edward Island	0.0	5.0	889	55.0	1,250
Nova Scotia	0.8	5.7	824	29.6	1,160
New Brunswick	3.4	6.4	819	29.6	1,240
Quebec	0.9	9.7	756	17.3	2,150
Ontario	0.8	9.2	890	18.6	2,050
Manitoba	0.6	7.7	817	18.4	1,570
Saskatchewan	0.0	4.6	743	13.1	975
Alberta	1.1	6.2	713	18.4	1,390
British Columbia	0.9	13.0	992	50.3	2,495

*Latest available year in each case.

TABLE IV—9

ESTIMATED PREVALENCE OF ALCOHOLISM IN CANADA, AND IN VARIOUS EUROPEAN
AND OTHER COUNTRIES*

(For sources and notes, see page 124.)

	Alcoholics per 100,000 population (20 years and older)	Year	Source
France	5,200	1954	Jellinek (1954)
United States	4,360	1955	Keller & Efron (1957)
Chile	2,960	1950	Popham (1956)
Sweden	2,580	1946	WHO (1951)
Switzerland	2,100	1953	Popham (1956)
Denmark	1,950	1948	WHO (1951)
Canada	1,890	1956	—
Norway	1,560	1947	WHO (1951)
Finland	1,430	1947	WHO (1951)
Australia	1,340	1947	WHO (1951)
England and Wales	1,100	1948	WHO (1951)
Italy	700	1954	Jellinek (1954)

*Latest available year in each case.

SOURCES AND NOTES

Table IV—1, A-K

The mortality data for Newfoundland (1949–1956), Quebec (1926–1956), and all remaining provinces (1921–1956) were obtained from the *Annual Reports on Vital Statistics* (Ottawa: Dominion Bureau of Statistics). These data applied to the calendar year, and were reported by place of occurrence from 1921 to 1943, and by place of residence from 1944 to 1956. Figures for Canada represent the total of the provincial figures shown in each year, and, therefore, are exclusive of the Yukon and Northwest Territories throughout, and of Newfoundland until 1949. Mortality data for Quebec, which were not reported by the Dominion Bureau until 1926, were obtained from another source (see below), and are included in the national totals shown for the years 1921 to 1925, inclusive. Accordingly, these totals differ from the figures reported for this period by the Dominion Bureau.

The sources employed to obtain mortality data other than that available in the reports of the Dominion Bureau of Statistics were as follows:

Nova Scotia 1909–1920: Annual Reports of the Registrar General, and of the Provincial Board of Health of Nova Scotia. These data applied to the year ending September 30. No vital statistics were reported for the year 1916.

Quebec, 1901–1925: Annual Reports of the Superior Board of Health (1901–1921), and of the Provincial Bureau of Health (1922–5) of Quebec. These data applied to the calendar year.

Ontario, 1901–1920: Annual Reports of the Registrar General of Ontario. These data applied to the calendar year. Deaths from cirrhosis of the liver were not separately reported prior to 1907, but were included in the general category of "diseases of the liver."

British Columbia, 1901–1920: Annual Reports of the Registrar General (1901–1913), and of the Provincial Board of Health (1914–1920) of British Columbia. These data applied to the calendar year with the exception of the period 1918 to 1920. The figures shown for 1918 apply to the six-month period from January 1 to June 30, and those for 1919 and 1920 to the year ending June 30.

Mortality data of the type included in this Table were also reported for a number of years prior to 1921 by the Governments of Saskatchewan and Alberta, and for a considerable period prior to 1949 by the Government of Newfoundland. However, the requisite documents were not available for utilization in connection with the present report. Parenthetically, with respect to vital statistics reported by provincial governments prior to the centralization and standardization of such reporting by the Dominion Bureau of Statistics, the following comments are especially noteworthy: ". . . legislation and methods differed widely; for instance, the international classification of deaths was not universally followed, and each province had its own scheme for the collection, compilation and presentation of results. Of the twenty-four items which the death certificate usually calls for, two provinces omitted sixteen, another fifteen, and another thirteen. Standards of administration, i.e., the degree of enforcement of registration, differed between provinces, and sometimes within the same province from year to year" (*First Annual Report on Vital Statistics, 1921*, Ottawa: Dominion Bureau of Statistics, 1923, p. v).

Deaths from alcoholism were not reported by the Dominion Bureau after 1949. The various shortcomings of reported mortality from this cause, as a measure of the

121

prevalence of alcoholism in a population, have been discussed by E. M. Jellinek, among others (see "Death from Alcoholism" in the United States in 1940, *Quart. J. Studies on Alcohol*, 3: 465–494, 1942). Particular cognizance should be taken of the strong probability that deaths from alcoholism tend to be severely under-reported owing to the stigma associated with the condition. Moreover, in many instances, the information necessary to make a diagnosis of alcoholism as the primary or underlying cause of death may not be available to the certifying physician.

For detailed discussions of the nature and extent of the apparent relationship between reported deaths from liver cirrhosis and the prevalence of alcoholism in North American and other countries see: Jolliffe, N. & Jellinek, E. M., Cirrhosis of the liver (*Effects of Alcohol on the Individual*, I, New Haven: Yale University Press, 1942, pp. 273–309), and Popham, R. E., The Jellinek Alcoholism Estimation Formula and its application to Canadian data (*Quart. J. Studies on Alcohol*, 17: 559–593, 1956).

Table IV—2

For the sources of the general mortality data included in this Table, see notes to Table IV—1, A-K. All figures are exclusive of stillbirths, and apply to the calendar year except as otherwise indicated in the notes to the latter Table. The data shown for Canada represent the total of available provincial figures in each year. A sex breakdown of the Canada totals for the years 1921 to 1925, inclusive, is not given since general mortality by sex was not obtained for these years for Quebec.

Table IV—3, A-K

Rates were calculated on the basis of the data in Table IV—1, A-K and Table IV—2, and population figures provided in Table V—1, A-K. Rates of death attributable to alcoholism, and to liver cirrhosis, were based on the population aged 20 and older, since the number of reported deaths from these causes is negligible among persons below this age. The rates shown for Canada were calculated on the basis of total available provincial mortality data in each year, and appropriately corrected population figures.

See also notes to Table IV—1, A-K.

Table IV—4

All data were obtained from the *Annual Reports on Mental Health Statistics* (formerly Mental Institutions), Ottawa: Dominion Bureau of Statistics. Figures apply to the calendar year, and are exclusive of the Yukon and Northwest Territories throughout, and of Newfoundland until 1949. Certain data were available for a few years prior to 1939, but these did not include figures for some of the categories of special interest in the present connection, and, therefore, were not utilized.

It should be kept in mind that generally only a small portion of all alcoholics in a population are likely to be admitted to mental hospitals; diagnostic criteria may differ from one institution to another, and from one period to another in the same institutions; and the annual reported frequency of first admissions may be affected, among other things, by changes in the number of institutions reporting, or in the duration of treatment. For a discussion of some of the principal factors which may have influenced trends in post-war admissions for alcoholism in Canada, see: Popham, R. E., Alcoholism admission trends analyzed (*Alcoholism Research*, 2 (4): 1–7, 1955).

122

Table IV—5
Percentages were calculated on the basis of the data provided in Table IV—4; rates were based on the admission figures given in the latter Table, and population data in Table V—1, A. Rates of first admission for alcoholism were based on the population aged 20 and older, since the number of admissions below this age is negligible.
See also notes to Table IV—4.

Table IV—6, A-J
All provincial data were obtained from the same source as the data for Canada (see notes to Table IV—4). Certain figures were available for a few years prior to 1950 in the case of all provinces except Newfoundland. However, these did not include admissions for "alcoholism without psychosis," and, therefore, were not tabulated.
See also notes to Table IV—4 and Table IV—5.

Table IV—7
Estimates were obtained by means of the Jellinek Alcoholism Estimation Formula, adapted for use with Canadian data. The method utilizes reported liver cirrhosis mortality, and was applied to data in Table IV—1, A-K, as follows: A = 172.92D for the period 1935–1949; and A = 213.24D for the period 1950–1956, where A is the number of alcoholics, and D is the centered two-year moving average of total reported deaths from liver cirrhosis for any given year. Different constants were employed for the two periods to allow for the effect of the Sixth Revision of the International Lists of Diseases and Causes of Death which was adopted in Canada in 1950. Parenthetically, to obtain alcoholism estimates for the years 1949 and 1950, it was necessary, for the same reason, to adjust the reported mortality figures in these years before calculating an average and applying the appropriate formula in each case.
Estimates are of the total alcoholic population; at present, it is not possible to obtain separate estimates for males and females in Canadian areas. The small discrepancies between the estimate shown for Canada and the sum of provincial estimates in certain years represent rounding errors. Figures for Canada are exclusive of the Yukon and Northwest Territories throughout, and of Newfoundland until 1950. Rates were calculated on the basis of population figures provided in Table V—1, A-K. The population of 20 years and older was employed since the occurrence of alcoholism below this age is negligible.
For detailed discussion of the nature and validity of the Jellinek Formula, and estimates based upon it, the reader is referred to: Popham, R. E., The Jellinek Alcoholism Estimation Formula and its application to Canadian data (*Quart. J. Studies on Alcohol*, 17: 559–593, 1956). However, it is important to stress here that the method is still open to question from many points of view, and is currently the object of further investigation. Studies to date suggest that the estimates shown are minimum, but that the formula probably should not be applied to mortality data reported in years prior to 1935.

Table IV—8
Sources and comments pertaining to the rates included in this summary Table may be found in the notes to Table IV—3, A-K, Table IV—5, Table IV—6, A-J, and Table IV—7.

123

Table IV—9

The sources of the estimates listed in th is Table were as follows:

Jellinek, E. M. International experience with the problems of alcoholism. Presented at the Alcoholism Research Symposium, Fifth International Congress on Mental Health. Toronto, 1954.

Keller, M. & Efron, V. Selected statistical tables on alcoholic beverages and on alcoholism. New Haven: J. Studies on Alcohol Inc., 1957.

Popham, R. E. The Jellinek Alcoholism Estimation Formula and its application to Canadian data. *Quart. J. Studies on Alcohol,* 17: 559–593, 1956.

World Health Organization, Expert Committee on Mental Health. *Report on the First Session of the Alcoholism Subcommittee.* Tech. Report Series, no. 42. Geneva, 1951.

All estimates were obtained by means of the Jellinek Alcoholism Estimation Formula as adapted for use in each country. See also notes to Table IV—7.

PART V

Census Populations and Intercensal Population Estimates

TABLE V–1

CENSUS POPULATION AND INTERCENSAL ESTIMATES OF THE POPULATION OF CANADA AND PROVINCES FOR ALL AGES, 15 YEARS AND OLDER, AND 20 YEARS AND OLDER BY SEX 1871–1956

(For sources and notes, see page 155.)

	Population of all ages (in thousands)			Population of 15 years and over (in thousands)			Population of 20 years and older (in thousands)		
	Total	Male	Female	Total	Male	Female	Total	Male	Female

A. Canada

Year	Total	Male	Female	Total	Male	Female	Total	Male	Female
1871	3,641	1,845	1,796	2,131	1,077	1,054	—	—	—
1872	3,705	1,878	1,827	2,179	1,101	1,078	—	—	—
1873	3,776	1,914	1,862	2,231	1,127	1,104	—	—	—
1874	3,844	1,948	1,896	2,282	1,153	1,129	—	—	—
1875	3,902	1,977	1,925	2,328	1,176	1,152	—	—	—
1876	3,957	2,004	1,953	2,372	1,198	1,174	—	—	—
1877	4,012	2,032	1,980	2,416	1,220	1,196	—	—	—
1878	4,067	2,059	2,008	2,461	1,242	1,219	—	—	—
1879	4,131	2,091	2,040	2,511	1,267	1,244	—	—	—
1880	4,200	2,126	2,074	2,565	1,294	1,271	—	—	—
1881	4,269	2,160.5	2,108.5	2,619	1,321	1,298	—	—	—
1882	4,315	2,184	2,131	2,657	1,341	1,316	—	—	—
1883	4,366	2,211	2,155	2,698	1,363	1,335	—	—	—
1884	4,418	2,239	2,179	2,741	1,385	1,356	—	—	—
1885	4,463	2,263	2,200	2,779	1,405	1,372	—	—	—
1886	4,502	2,283	2,219	2,814	1,424	1,390	—	—	—
1887	4,544	2,306	2,238	2,850	1,445	1,405	—	—	—
1888	4,592	2,331	2,261	2,891	1,467	1,424	—	—	—
1889	4,638	2,356	2,282	2,931	1,488	1,443	—	—	—
1890	4,684	2,380	2,304	2,968	1,508	1,460	—	—	—
1891	4,734	2,407	2,327	3,013	1,532	1,481	—	—	—
1892	4,773	2,428	2,345	3,047	1,550	1,497	—	—	—
1893	4,810	2,448	2,362	3,080	1,568	1,512	—	—	—
1894	4,847	2,467	2,380	3,113	1,585	1,528	—	—	—
1895	4,883	2,487	2,396	3,145	1,602	1,543	—	—	—
1896	4,920	2,507	2,413	3,179	1,620	1,559	—	—	—
1897	4,959	2,528	2,431	3,214	1,639	1,575	—	—	—

TABLE V—1 (continued)

Year	Population of all ages (in thousands)			Population of 15 years and over (in thousands)			Population of 20 years and older (in thousands)		
	Total	Male	Female	Total	Male	Female	Total	Male	Female
A. Canada (continued)									
1898	5,002	2,551	2,451	3,251	1,659	1,592	—	—	—
1899	5,052	2,557	2,475	3,294	1,681	1,613	—	—	—
1900	5,108	2,607	2,501	3,340	1,706	1,634	—	—	—
1901	5,324	2,718.5	2,605.5	3,484	1,786	1,698	2,930	1,506	1,424
1902	5,450	2,793	2,657	3,575	1,844	1,731	3,013	1,557	1,456
1903	5,611	2,887	2,724	3,689	1,914	1,775	3,116	1,620	1,496
1904	5,789	2,990	2,799	3,815	1,990	1,825	3,229	1,689	1,540
1905	5,966	3,093	2,873	3,940	2,066	1,874	3,342	1,759	1,583
1906	6,066	3,156	2,910	4,016	2,118	1,898	3,413	1,808	1,605
1907	6,381	3,333	3,048	4,235	2,246	1,989	3,606	1,922	1,684
1908	6,599	3,460	3,139	4,390	2,341	2,049	3,745	2,008	1,737
1909	6,777	3,566	3,211	4,519	2,423	2,096	3,863	2,084	1,779
1910	6,968	3,680	3,288	4,658	2,511	2,147	3,989	2,165	1,824
1911	7,191	3,811.5	3,379.5	4,819	2,612	2,207	4,134	2,257.5	1,876.5
1912	7,373	3,898	3,475	4,930	2,662	2,268	4,231	2,301	1,930
1913	7,617	4,015	3,602	5,082	2,733	2,349	4,364	2,364	2,000
1914	7,863	4,133	3,730	5,235	2,804	2,431	4,497	2,426	2,071
1915	7,965	4,175	3,790	5,292	2,824	2,468	4,546	2,442	2,104
1916	7,986	4,174	3,812	5,294	2,814	2,480	4,550	2,434	2,116
1917	8,046	4,194	3,852	5,323	2,818	2,505	4,576	2,438	2,138
1918	8,134	4,228	3,906	5,369	2,831	2,538	4,616	2,449	2,167
1919	8,298	4,301	3,997	5,466	2,871	2,595	4,701	2,484	2,217
1920	8,543	4,415	4,128	5,615	2,937	2,678	4,830	2,541	2,289
1921	8,776	4,523	4,253	5,756	2,999	2,757	4,953	2,595	2,358
1922	8,907	4,579	4,328	5,863	3,043.5	2,819.5	5,043	2,633	2,410
1923	8,998	4,615	4,383	5,942	3,073.5	2,868.5	5,107	2,655.5	2,451.5
1924	9,131	4,672	4,459	6,050	3,119	2,931	5,196	2,692	2,504
1925	9,282	4,737.5	4,544.5	6,174	3,173	3,001	5,298	2,736	2,562
1926	9,439	4,806.5	4,632.5	6,298	3,227.5	3,070.5	5,399	2,779.5	2,619.5
1927	9,624	4,919	4,705	6,457	3,323	3,134	5,534	2,861	2,673
1928	9,822	5,038	4,784	6,627	3,426.5	3,200.5	5,675	2,949	2,726
1929	10,016	5,154.5	4,861.5	6,791	3,527.5	3,263.5	5,808	3,033	2,775

TABLE V—1 (continued)

	Population of all ages (in thousands)			Population of 15 years and over (in thousands)			Population of 20 years and older (in thousands)		
	Total	Male	Female	Total	Male	Female	Total	Male	Female
A. Canada (continued)									
1930	10,195	5,264	4,931	6,943	3,622	3,321	5,931	3,111	2,820
1931	10,363	5,366.5	4,996.5	7,086	3,710	3,376	6,047	3,185	2,862
1932	10,496	5,431.5	5,064.5	7,216	3,773.5	3,442.5	6,169	3,245	2,924
1933	10,619	5,491	5,128	7,332	3,829.5	3,502.5	6,294	3,305	2,989
1934	10,727	5,541.5	5,185.5	7,449	3,885	3,564	6,411	3,360	3,051
1935	10,829	5,527.5	5,241.5	7,563	3,936.5	3,626.5	6,523	3,411	3,112
1936	10,934	5,636	5,298	7,693	3,996.5	3,696.5	6,627	3,458	3,169
1937	11,029	5,678.5	5,350.5	7,815	4,053.5	3,761.5	6,728	3,504.5	3,223.5
1938	11,136	5,729	5,407	7,945	4,113.5	3,831.5	6,835	3,554	3,281
1939	11,250	5,781.5	5,468.5	8,069	4,171.5	3,897.5	6,947	3,606	3,341
1940	11,364	5,834	5,530	8,190	4,226.5	3,963.5	7,061	3,657.5	3,403.5
1941	11,490	5,890.5	5,599.5	8,297	4,274	4,023	7,178	3,710	3,468
1942	11,637	5,961.5	5,675.5	8,423	4,333.5	4,089.5	7,316	3,776	3,540
1943	11,778	6,030	5,748	8,532	4,384	4,148	7,436	3,831	3,605
1944	11,929	6,102.5	5,826.5	8,642	4,431	4,211	7,549	3,878.5	3,670.5
1945	12,055	6,144.5	5,910.5	8,725	4,456	4,269	7,639	3,908	3,731
1946	12,268	6,246.5	6,021.5	8,854	4,510.5	4,343.5	7,779	3,970	3,809
1947	12,527	6,374.5	6,152.5	8,995	4,575.5	4,419.5	7,927	4,038	3,889
1948	12,779	6,513	6,286	9,128	4,640	4,488	8,068	4,106	3,962
1949	13,423	6,819.5	6,603.5	9,493	4,816.5	4,676.5	8,408	4,269	4,139
1950	13,688	6,941.5	6,746.5	9,625	4,872.5	4,752.5	8,551	4,330.5	4,220.5
1951	13,984	7,074	6,910	9,742	4,910.5	4,831.5	8,686	4,379.5	4,306.5
1952	14,405	7,301	7,104	9,985	5,044.5	4,940.5	8,917	4,504	4,413
1953	14,756	7,474.5	7,281.5	10,161	5,129	5,032	9,081	4,581	4,500
1954	15,168	7,683	7,485	10,377	5,235.5	5,141.5	9,274	4,675	4,599
1955	15,573	7,883	7,690	10,560	5,322.5	5,237.5	9,431	4,748	4,683
1956	15,941	8,063	7,878	10,738	5,405.5	5,332.5	9,577	4,814	4,763
B. Newfoundland									
1949	345	176	169	222	114	108	189	97.5	91.5
1950	351	180	171	223	115	108	190	98	92
1951	361	185	176	220	113	107	190	98	92

TABLE V—1 (continued)

	Population of all ages (in thousands)			Population of 15 years and over (in thousands)			Population of 20 years and older (in thousands)		
	Total	Male	Female	Total	Male	Female	Total	Male	Female
B. Newfoundland (continued)									
1952	374	192	182	227	117	110	196	102	94
1953	383	197	186	231	119	112	199	103	96
1954	398	205	193	239	124	115	206	107	99
1955	412	212	200	246	127.5	118.5	212	110	102
1956	424	219	205	251	130	121	216	112	104
C. Prince Edward Island									
1871	94	—	—	58	29	29	—	—	—
1872	96	—	—	59	29	30	—	—	—
1873	98	—	—	60	30	30	—	—	—
1874	99	—	—	61	30	31	—	—	—
1875	101	—	—	62	31	31	—	—	—
1876	102	—	—	63	31	32	—	—	—
1877	103	—	—	63	31	32	—	—	—
1878	104	—	—	64	32	32	—	—	—
1879	105	—	—	65	32	33	—	—	—
1880	107	—	—	66	33	33	—	—	—
1881	109	—	—	67	33	34	—	—	—
1882	109	—	—	67	33	34	—	—	—
1883	109	—	—	67	33	34	—	—	—
1884	109	—	—	67	33	34	—	—	—
1885	109	—	—	68	33	34	—	—	—
1886	109	—	—	68	34	34	—	—	—
1887	109	—	—	68	34	34	—	—	—
1888	109	—	—	68	34	34	—	—	—
1889	109	—	—	68	34	34	—	—	—
1890	109	—	—	68	34	34	—	—	—
1891	109	—	—	68	34	34	—	—	—
1892	108	—	—	68	34	34	—	—	—
1893	108	—	—	68	34	34	—	—	—

TABLE V—1 (*continued*)

C. Prince Edward Island (*continued*)

	Population of all ages (in thousands)			Population of 15 years and over (in thousands)			Population of 20 years and older (in thousands)		
	Total	Male	Female	Total	Male	Female	Total	Male	Female
1894	107	—	—	68	34	34	—	—	—
1895	106	—	—	67	33	34	—	—	—
1896	105	—	—	67	33	34	—	—	—
1897	104	—	—	67	33	34	—	—	—
1898	104	—	—	67	33	34	—	—	—
1899	103	—	—	66	33	33	—	—	—
1900	103	—	—	67	33	34	—	—	—
1901	103	52	51	67	33	34	55	27	28
1902	101	51	50	66	33	33	54	27	27
1903	100	50	50	65	32	33	54	27	27
1904	99	50	49	65	32	33	54	27	27
1905	99	50	49	65	32	33	54	27	27
1906	96	48	48	65	32	33	53	26	27
1907	96	48	48	64	32	32	53	26	27
1908	95	48	47	63	31	32	53	26	27
1909	94	47	47	63	31	32	52	26	26
1910	94	47	47	63	31	32	53	26	27
1911	94	47	47	63	31	32	53	26	27
1912	94	47	47	63	31	32	53	26	27
1913	94	47	47	63	31	32	53	26	27
1914	95	48	47	64	32	32	54	27	27
1915	94	47	47	63	31	32	53	26	27
1916	92	46	46	62	31	31	52	26	26
1917	90	45	45	61	30	31	51	26	25
1918	89	45	44	60	30	30	51	26	25
1919	89	45	44	60	30	30	51	26	25
1920	89	45	44	60	30	30	51	26	25
1921	89	45	44	60	30	30	51	26	25
1922	89	45	44	60	30.5	29.5	52	26	26
1923	87	44	43	59	29	30	50	25	25
1924	86	43	43	58	29	29	50	25	25
1925	86	43	43	58	29	29	50	25	25

TABLE V–1 (continued)

	Population of all ages (in thousands)			Population of 15 years and over (in thousands)			Population of 20 years and older (in thousands)		
	Total	Male	Female	Total	Male	Female	Total	Male	Female
	C. Prince Edward Island (continued)								
1926	87	44	43	59	30	29	50	25	25
1927	87	44	43	59	30	29	50	25	25
1928	88	45	43	60	31	29	51	26	25
1929	88	45	43	60	31	29	51	26	25
1930	88	45	43	60	31	29	51	26	25
1931	88	45	43	60	31	29	51	26.5	24.5
1932	89	46	43	61	32	29	52	27	25
1933	90	46	44	62	32	30	53	28	25
1934	91	47	44	63	33	30	54	28	26
1935	92	47.5	44.5	65	34	31	55	28.5	26.5
1936	93	48	45	66	34	32	57	29.5	27.5
1937	93	48	45	65	34	31	56	29	27
1938	94	49	45	67	35	32	57	30	27
1939	94	49	45	66	34	32	57	30	27
1940	95	49	46	67	35	32	58	30.5	27.5
1941	95	49	46	66	34.5	31.5	57	30	27
1942	90	47	43	63	33	30	54	29	25
1943	91	47	44	64	34	30	55	29	26
1944	91	47	44	64	34	30	55	29	26
1945	92	48	44	65	34	31	56	29	27
1946	94	48	46	66	34	32	57	29.5	27.5
1947	94	48	46	66	34	32	57	29	28
1948	93	48	45	64	33	31	55	28	27
1949	94	49	45	64	33	31	55	29	26
1950	96	49	47	65	34	31	56	29	27
1951	98	50	48	66	34	32	57	29	28
1952	103	52	51	68	34	34	60	30	30
1953	106	54	52	70	35	35	61	30.5	30.5
1954	105	53	52	69	35	34	61	31	30
1955	108	55	53	71	36	35	63	32	31
1956	105	53	52	69	35	34	60	30.5	29.5

TABLE V—1 (continued)

	Population of all ages (in thousands)			Population of 15 years and over (in thousands)			Population of 20 years and older (in thousands)		
	Total	Male	Female	Total	Male	Female	Total	Male	Female

D. Nova Scotia

	Total	Male	Female	Total	Male	Female	Total	Male	Female
1871	388	—	—	235	116	119	—	—	—
1872	394	—	—	239	118	121	—	—	—
1873	400	—	—	244	120	124	—	—	—
1874	406	—	—	248	122	126	—	—	—
1875	411	—	—	252	124	128	—	—	—
1876	415	—	—	255	126	129	—	—	—
1877	420	—	—	258	127	131	—	—	—
1878	425	—	—	262	129	133	—	—	—
1879	430	—	—	266	131	135	—	—	—
1880	435	—	—	270	133	137	—	—	—
1881	441	—	—	274	135.5	138.5	—	—	—
1882	442	—	—	276	137	139	—	—	—
1883	443	—	—	277	137	140	—	—	—
1884	445	—	—	280	139	141	—	—	—
1885	446	—	—	281	140	141	—	—	—
1886	446	—	—	282	140	142	—	—	—
1887	446	—	—	283	141	142	—	—	—
1888	447	—	—	285	142	143	—	—	—
1889	448	—	—	287	143	144	—	—	—
1890	449	—	—	288	144	144	—	—	—
1891	450	—	—	290	145	145	—	—	—
1892	451	—	—	291	146	145	—	—	—
1893	452	—	—	293	147	146	—	—	—
1894	452	—	—	294	148	146	—	—	—
1895	452	—	—	294	148	146	—	—	—
1896	453	—	—	296	149	147	—	—	—
1897	454	—	—	297	150	147	—	—	—
1898	455	—	—	298	151	147	—	—	—
1899	457	—	—	301	153	148	—	—	—
1900	459	—	—	303	154	149	—	—	—
1901	460	234	226	304	155	149	255	129.5	125.5

TABLE V—1 (continued)

	Population of all ages (in thousands)			Population of 15 years and over (in thousands)			Population of 20 years and older (in thousands)		
	Total	Male	Female	Total	Male	Female	Total	Male	Female

D. Nova Scotia (continued)

	Total	Male	Female	Total	Male	Female	Total	Male	Female
1902	459	234	225	303	155	148	255	130	125
1903	460	234	226	304	155	149	256	130	126
1904	463	236	227	306	156	150	258	131	127
1905	464	236	228	307	157	150	258	132	126
1906	465	237	228	308	157	151	259	132	127
1907	475	242	233	314	161	153	265	135	130
1908	480	245	235	318	163	155	268	137	131
1909	483	246	237	320	164	156	270	138	132
1910	486	248	238	322	165	157	272	139	133
1911	492	251	241	326	167	159	276	141.5	134.5
1912	496	253	243	329	168	161	278	142	136
1913	504	257	247	334	171	163	283	145	138
1914	512	261	251	339	173	166	287	147	140
1915	511	260	251	338	173	165	287	147	140
1916	505	257	248	334	171	163	283	145	138
1917	503	256	247	333	170	163	282	144	138
1918	502	256	246	332	169	163	282	144	138
1919	507	258	249	335	171	164	284	145	139
1920	516	263	253	341	174	167	290	148	142
1921	524	267	257	346	176	170	294	150	144
1922	522	266	256	345	176	169	293	149.5	143.5
1923	518	264	254	343	175	168	291	149	142
1924	516	263	253	343	175	168	291	149	142
1925	515	263	252	343	175.5	168	291	149	142
1926	515	263	252	343	175.5	167.5	292	149.5	142.5
1927	515	263	252	344	176	168	292	149.5	142.5
1928	515	263	252	345	177	168	293	150.5	142.5
1929	515	264	251	346	178	168	293	151	142
1930	514	263.5	250.5	346	178	168	293	151	142
1931	513	263	250	346	178.5	167.5	293	151	142
1932	519	266	253	352	181.5	170.5	297	153.5	143.5

TABLE V—1 (continued)

	Population of all ages (in thousands)			Population of 15 years and over (in thousands)			Population of 20 years and older (in thousands)		
	Total	Male	Female	Total	Male	Female	Total	Male	Female

D. Nova Scotia (continued)

1933	525	269	256	358	185	173	304	157	147
1934	531	272.5	258.5	364	188	176	310	160	150
1935	536	275	261	371	191	180	317	164	153
1936	543	279	264	379	195.5	183.5	324	168	156
1937	549	282	267	386	199	187	329	170	159
1938	555	285	270	392	202	190	335	173	162
1939	561	288	273	397	204	193	340	175	165
1940	569	292	277	404	208	196	347	179	168
1941	578	296	282	409	210	199	353	182	171
1942	591	302	289	419	215	204	363	187	176
1943	606	310	296	430	220	210	374	192	182
1944	611	312	299	432	221	211	377	193	184
1945	619	315	304	436	222	214	381	194	187
1946	608	310	298	427	217	210	374	190	184
1947	615	312.5	302.5	430	218	212	377	191.5	185.5
1948	625	318	307	432	219	213	379	192	187
1949	629	319	310	432	218	214	379	191.5	187.5
1950	638	324	314	435	220	215	383	194	189
1951	643	325	318	433	218	215	382	192.5	189.5
1952	653	330.5	322.5	438	221	217	386	195	191
1953	663	336	327	443	223.5	219.5	391	197.5	193.5
1954	673	342.5	330.5	448	226.5	221.5	395	199.5	195.5
1955	683	347	336	454	230	224	400	202	198
1956	696	354	342	460	233	227	405	205	200

E. New Brunswick

1871	286	—	—	169	86	83	—	—	—
1872	290	—	—	172	88	84	—	—	—
1873	294	—	—	175	89	86	—	—	—
1874	298	—	—	178	91	87	—	—	—

TABLE V—1 (continued)

E. New Brunswick (continued)

	Population of all ages (in thousands)			Population of 15 years and over (in thousands)			Population of 20 years and older (in thousands)		
	Total	Male	Female	Total	Male	Female	Total	Male	Female
1875	301	—	—	181	92	89	—	—	—
1876	304	—	—	183	93	90	—	—	—
1877	307	—	—	186	95	91	—	—	—
1878	310	—	—	188	96	92	—	—	—
1879	313	—	—	191	97	94	—	—	—
1880	317	—	—	195	99	96	—	—	—
1881	321	—	—	197	100	97	—	—	—
1882	321	—	—	197	100	97	—	—	—
1883	321	—	—	198	100	98	—	—	—
1884	321	—	—	199	101	98	—	—	—
1885	321	—	—	199	101	98	—	—	—
1886	321	—	—	200	101	99	—	—	—
1887	321	—	—	201	102	99	—	—	—
1888	321	—	—	201	102	99	—	—	—
1889	321	—	—	202	102	100	—	—	—
1890	321	—	—	202	102	100	—	—	—
1891	321	—	—	203	103	100	—	—	—
1892	322	—	—	204	103	101	—	—	—
1893	323	—	—	205	104	101	—	—	—
1894	323	—	—	205	104	101	—	—	—
1895	323	—	—	206	104	102	—	—	—
1896	324	—	—	207	105	102	—	—	—
1897	325	—	—	208	105	103	—	—	—
1898	326	—	—	209	105	104	—	—	—
1899	327	—	—	210	106	104	—	—	—
1900	329	—	—	211	107	104	—	—	—
1901	331	169	162	213	108	105	177	89.5	87.5
1902	331	169	162	213	108	105	177	90	87
1903	331	169	162	213	108	105	178	90	88
1904	333	170	163	215	110	105	179	91	88
1905	333	170	163	214	109	105	179	91	88
1906	334	171	163	215	109	106	180	92	88

TABLE V—1 *(continued)*

	Population of all ages (in thousands)			Population of 15 years and over (in thousands)			Population of 20 years and older (in thousands)		
	Total	Male	Female	Total	Male	Female	Total	Male	Female
			E. New Brunswick *(continued)*						
1907	341	174	167	220	112	108	184	94	90
1908	345	176	169	222	113	109	186	95	91
1909	346	177	169	223	114	109	187	96	91
1910	348	178	170	224	114	110	189	97	92
1911	352	180	172	227	116	111	191	98	93
1912	356	182	174	229	117	112	193	99	94
1913	363	185	178	234	120	114	197	101	96
1914	371	189	182	239	122	117	201	103	98
1915	371	189	182	238	122	116	201	103	98
1916	368	188	180	236	121	115	199	102	97
1917	368	187	181	236	121	115	199	102	97
1918	369	188	181	236	121	115	199	102	97
1919	373	190	183	239	122	117	201	103	98
1920	381	194	187	248	127	121	205	105	100
1921	388	197	191	248	126.5	121.5	209	107	102
1922	389	198	191	249	127	122	210	107.5	102.5
1923	389	198	191	249	127	122	210	107	103
1924	391	199	192	251	128	123	212	108	104
1925	393	200	193	252	128.5	123.5	213	109	104
1926	396	202	194	255	130	125	215	109.5	105.5
1927	398	203	195	257	131	126	216	110	106
1928	401	204	197	259	132	127	218	111	107
1929	404	206	198	261	133.5	127.5	219	112	107
1930	406	207	199	262	134	128	220	113	107
1931	408	208.5	199.5	263	135	128	221	113.5	107.5
1932	414	211.5	202.5	268	138	130	224	115	109
1933	419	214	205	273	140	133	229	118	111
1934	423	216	207	277	142.5	134.5	233	120	113
1935	428	219	209	283	146	137	239	123	116
1936	433	222	211	289	149	140	244	126	118
1937	437	224	213	294	151.5	142.5	247	128	119
1938	442	226	216	299	154	145	251	129.5	121.5

TABLE V—1 (*continued*)

	Population of all ages (in thousands)			Population of 15 years and over (in thousands)			Population of 20 years and older (in thousands)		
	Total	Male	Female	Total	Male	Female	Total	Male	Female
E. New Brunswick (*continued*)									
1939	447	229	218	303	156	147	255	132	123
1940	452	231	221	308	159	149	259	134	125
1941	457	234	223	312	161	151	263	136	127
1942	464	237	227	317	163	154	269	139	130
1943	463	237	226	316	163	153	269	139	130
1944	461	236.5	224.5	315	162.5	152.5	269	139	130
1945	467	239	228	318	163	155	273	140.5	132.5
1946	478	243.5	234.5	324	165	159	278	142.5	135.5
1947	488	248	240	327	166.5	160.5	282	144	138
1948	498	253.5	244.5	331	168	163	286	145.5	140.5
1949	508	258	250	335	169	166	290	147	143
1950	512	259	253	334	168	166	290	146.5	143.5
1951	516	259	257	332	166	166	289	144.5	144.5
1952	526	265	261	337	168	169	294	147	147
1953	536	269.5	266.5	341	170	171	298	148	150
1954	547	275	272	347	172	175	303	150	153
1955	558	281	277	353	175.5	177.5	308	153	155
1956	569	286	283	361	180	181	314	157	157
F. Quebec									
1871	1,191	—	—	692	343	349	—	—	—
1872	1,208	—	—	704	349	355	—	—	—
1873	1,227	—	—	717	355	362	—	—	—
1874	1,246	—	—	730	362	368	—	—	—
1875	1,260	—	—	741	367	374	—	—	—
1876	1,275	—	—	751	372	379	—	—	—
1877	1,289	—	—	762	377	385	—	—	—
1878	1,304	—	—	773	382	391	—	—	—
1879	1,322	—	—	786	389	397	—	—	—
1880	1,341	—	—	799	395	404	—	—	—
1881	1,360	—	—	813	402	411	—	—	—

TABLE V—1 (continued)

F. Quebec (continued)

Year	Population of all ages (in thousands)			Population of 15 years and over (in thousands)			Population of 20 years and older (in thousands)		
	Total	Male	Female	Total	Male	Female	Total	Male	Female
1882	1,372	—	—	821	406	415	—	—	—
1883	1,386	—	—	831	411	420	—	—	—
1884	1,401	—	—	841	416	425	—	—	—
1885	1,414	—	—	849	420	429	—	—	—
1886	1,424	—	—	856	424	432	—	—	—
1887	1,436	—	—	865	429	436	—	—	—
1888	1,449	—	—	874	433	441	—	—	—
1889	1,462	—	—	883	438	445	—	—	—
1890	1,475	—	—	891	442	449	—	—	—
1891	1,489	—	—	901	447	454	—	—	—
1892	1,504	—	—	911	452	459	—	—	—
1893	1,518	—	—	921	457	464	—	—	—
1894	1,532	—	—	931	463	468	—	—	—
1895	1,546	—	—	940	467	473	—	—	—
1896	1,560	—	—	950	472	478	—	—	—
1897	1,575	—	—	961	478	483	—	—	—
1898	1,591	—	—	972	483	489	—	—	—
1899	1,610	—	—	985	491	494	—	—	—
1900	1,630	—	—	998	497	501	—	—	—
1901	1,649	824	825	1,011	504	507	840	418	422
1902	1,670	835	835	1,024	511	513	852	425	427
1903	1,709	856	853	1,049	525	524	872	436	436
1904	1,752	878	874	1,076	540	536	895	448	447
1905	1,771	889	882	1,087	546	541	906	455	451
1906	1,784	896	888	1,097	552	545	914	460	454
1907	1,853	932	921	1,138	573	565	950	479	471
1908	1,902	957	945	1,170	591	579	976	493	483
1909	1,931	973	958	1,187	600	587	992	502	490
1910	1,965	991	974	1,208	610	598	1,011	513	498
1911	2,006	1,013	993	1,234	626	608	1,033	525	508
1912	2,042	1,030	1,012	1,257	629	628	1,052	534	518

TABLE V—1 (continued)

F. Quebec (continued)

	Population of all ages (in thousands)			Population of 15 years and over (in thousands)			Population of 20 years and older (in thousands)		
	Total	Male	Female	Total	Male	Female	Total	Male	Female
1913	2,096	1,056	1,040	1,291	647	644	1,080	547	533
1914	2,148	1,081	1,067	1,324	665	659	1,106	559	547
1915	2,162	1,087	1,075	1,333	670	663	1,114	562	552
1916	2,154	1,082	1,072	1,329	669	660	1,110	560	550
1917	2,169	1,088	1,081	1,339	673	666	1,118	563	555
1918	2,191	1,098	1,093	1,353	679	674	1,129	568	561
1919	2,234	1,119	1,115	1,381	692	689	1,151	578	573
1920	2,299	1,150	1,149	1,421	711	710	1,185	594	591
1921	2,361	1,180	1,181	1,461	730	731	1,217	609.5	607.5
1922	2,409	1,199.5	1,209.5	1,497	744	753	1,249	622	627
1923	2,446	1,214	1,232	1,527	756	771	1,276	633	643
1924	2,495	1,235	1,260	1,562	770	792	1,307	646	661
1925	2,549	1,258.5	1,290.5	1,601	786.5	814.5	1,342	661	681
1926	2,603	1,280.5	1,322.5	1,637	800	837	1,373	673.5	699.5
1927	2,657	1,313	1,344	1,682	827	855	1,411	695.5	715.5
1928	2,715	1,346	1,369	1,728	854	874	1,449	718	731
1929	2,772	1,383	1,389	1,771	882	889	1,485	742	743
1930	2,825	1,416	1,409	1,813	909	904	1,518	763.5	754.5
1931	2,875	1,447.5	1,427.5	1,852	933	919	1,552	786	766
1932	2,925	1,476	1,449	1,902	961	941	1,601	812	789
1933	2,972	1,498	1,474	1,936	977	959	1,634	826.5	807.5
1934	3,016	1,519	1,497	1,970	992	978	1,666	841	825
1935	3,057	1,535	1,522	1,995	1,001	994	1,687	847.5	839.5
1936	3,099	1,555	1,544	2,025	1,015	1,010	1,706	856	850
1937	3,141	1,574	1,567	2,072	1,037	1,035	1,746	874	872
1938	3,183	1,596	1,587	2,120	1,061	1,059	1,786	895	891
1939	3,230	1,621	1,609	2,173	1,089	1,084	1,832	919	913
1940	3,278	1,645	1,633	2,221	1,112.5	1,108.5	1,873	939	934
1941	3,332	1,673	1,659	2,269	1,137	1,132	1,918	961	957
1942	3,390	1,702	1,688	2,316	1,160	1,156	1,964	984	980
1943	3,457	1,736	1,721	2,366	1,184	1,182	2,012	1,006	1,006

TABLE V–1 (continued)

Year	Population of all ages (in thousands)			Population of 15 years and over (in thousands)			Population of 20 years and older (in thousands)		
	Total	Male	Female	Total	Male	Female	Total	Male	Female
F. Quebec (continued)									
1944	3,500	1,758	1,742	2,399	1,199.5	1,199.5	2,044	1,020	1,024
1945	3,560	1,786	1,774	2,436	1,218	1,218	2,082	1,039	1,043
1946	3,629	1,820	1,809	2,478	1,237	1,241	2,126	1,060	1,066
1947	3,710	1,861	1,849	2,522	1,258	1,264	2,172	1,082	1,090
1948	3,788	1,899	1,889	2,559	1,274	1,285	2,211	1,100	1,111
1949	3,882	1,944	1,938	2,607	1,297	1,310	2,262	1,124	1,138
1950	3,969	1,987.5	1,981.5	2,652	1,316	1,336	2,309	1,145	1,164
1951	4,056	2,022	2,034	2,690	1,326	1,364	2,352	1,158.5	1,193.5
1952	4,174	2,087	2,087	2,764	1,368	1,396	2,423	1,197.5	1,225.5
1953	4,269	2,135	2,134	2,818	1,395	1,423	2,474	1,221	1,253
1954	4,388	2,195	2,193	2,886	1,429	1,457	2,535	1,251.5	1,283.5
1955	4,520	2,262	2,258	2,944	1,458	1,486	2,584	1,275	1,309
1956	4,634	2,318	2,316	3,006	1,487	1,519	2,635	1,299	1,336
G. Ontario									
1871	1,621	—	—	937	480	457	—	—	—
1872	1,651	—	—	961	492	469	—	—	—
1873	1,685	—	—	988	505	483	—	—	—
1874	1,718	—	—	1,015	518	497	—	—	—
1875	1,746	—	—	1,039	530	509	—	—	—
1876	1,774	—	—	1,063	542	521	—	—	—
1877	1,802	—	—	1,087	553	534	—	—	—
1878	1,829	—	—	1,111	565	546	—	—	—
1879	1,861	—	—	1,138	578	560	—	—	—
1880	1,894	—	—	1,166	592	574	—	—	—
1881	1,927	—	—	1,195	606	589	—	—	—
1882	1,946	—	—	1,213	615	598	—	—	—
1883	1,968	—	—	1,234	625	609	—	—	—
1884	1,988	—	—	1,253	634	619	—	—	—
1885	2,005	—	—	1,271	643	628	—	—	—
1886	2,020	—	—	1,288	651	637	—	—	—

TABLE V—1 (continued)

G. Ontario (continued)

Year	Population of all ages (in thousands) Total	Male	Female	Population of 15 years and over (in thousands) Total	Male	Female	Population of 20 years and older (in thousands) Total	Male	Female
1887	2,037	—	—	1,305	660	645	—	—	—
1888	2,057	—	—	1,325	669	656	—	—	—
1889	2,075	—	—	1,344	679	665	—	—	—
1890	2,093	—	—	1,363	688	675	—	—	—
1891	2,114	—	—	1,384	698	686	—	—	—
1892	2,119	—	—	1,394	702	692	—	—	—
1893	2,122	—	—	1,403	706	697	—	—	—
1894	2,128	—	—	1,413	711	702	—	—	—
1895	2,133	—	—	1,423	715	708	—	—	—
1896	2,137	—	—	1,433	720	713	—	—	—
1897	2,142	—	—	1,443	724	719	—	—	—
1898	2,149	—	—	1,454	729	725	—	—	—
1899	2,159	—	—	1,468	735	733	—	—	—
1900	2,172	—	—	1,484	743	741	—	—	—
1901	2,183	1,097	1,086	1,498	749	749	1,268	634	634
1902	2,194	1,105	1,089	1,510	758	752	1,281	643	638
1903	2,217	1,119	1,098	1,530	770	760	1,301	655	646
1904	2,246	1,137	1,109	1,556	787	769	1,325	670	655
1905	2,289	1,161	1,128	1,590	806	784	1,358	689	669
1906	2,299	1,169	1,130	1,602	816	786	1,371	698	673
1907	2,365	1,206	1,159	1,652	844	808	1,417	724	693
1908	2,412	1,233	1,179	1,691	867	824	1,453	746	707
1909	2,444	1,252	1,192	1,717	883	834	1,479	762	717
1910	2,482	1,275	1,207	1,749	903	846	1,510	781	729
1911	2,527	1,301	1,226	1,786	925	861	1,545	801.5	743.5
1912	2,572	1,322	1,250	1,815	938	877	1,572	813	759
1913	2,639	1,353	1,286	1,861	959	902	1,613	832	781
1914	2,705	1,385	1,320	1,905	979	926	1,653	850	803
1915	2,724	1,392	1,332	1,916	982	934	1,665	855	810
1916	2,713	1,383	1,330	1,906	975	931	1,657	848	809
1917	2,724	1,386	1,338	1,911	975	936	1,664	849	815
1918	2,744	1,394	1,350	1,923	978	945	1,677	854	823

TABLE V—1 (continued)

G. Ontario (continued)

Year	Population of all ages (in thousands) Total	Male	Female	Population of 15 years and over (in thousands) Total	Male	Female	Population of 20 years and older (in thousands) Total	Male	Female
1919	2,789	1,414	1,375	1,952	991	961	1,705	866	839
1920	2,863	1,449	1,414	2,000	1,012	988	1,750	886	864
1921	2,934	1,482	1,452	2,048	1,033.5	1,014.5	1,793	905.5	887.5
1922	2,980	1,501	1,479	2,089	1,051	1,038	1,829	921	908
1923	3,013	1,513	1,500	2,117	1,060.5	1,056.5	1,852	928	924
1924	3,059	1,532	1,527	2,156	1,076.5	1,079.5	1,886	942	944
1925	3,111	1,553	1,558	2,201	1,094	1,107	1,924	956	968
1926	3,164	1,576	1,588	2,247	1,114	1,133	1,964	973	991
1927	3,219	1,612	1,607	2,293	1,144	1,149	2,006	1,000	1,006
1928	3,278	1,651.5	1,626.5	2,344	1,179	1,165	2,049	1,030	1,019
1929	3,334	1,685.5	1,648.5	2,392	1,209	1,183	2,088	1,055	1,033
1930	3,386	1,719	1,667	2,435	1,237	1,198	2,123	1,078	1,045
1931	3,432	1,749	1,683	2,473	1,262.5	1,210.5	2,154	1,099	1,055
1932	3,473	1,768	1,705	2,509	1,279.5	1,229.5	2,189	1,116	1,073
1933	3,512	1,788	1,724	2,547	1,299	1,248	2,233	1,139	1,094
1934	3,544	1,804	1,740	2,585	1,318.5	1,266.5	2,273	1,159	1,114
1935	3,575	1,820.5	1,754.5	2,626	1,339	1,287	2,316	1,181.5	1,134.5
1936	3,606	1,840	1,766	2,674	1,367	1,307	2,357	1,205	1,152
1937	3,637	1,851	1,786	2,710	1,380.5	1,329.5	2,384	1,215	1,169
1938	3,672	1,868	1,804	2,751	1,400	1,351	2,416	1,230	1,186
1939	3,708	1,884.5	1,823.5	2,788	1,417.5	1,370.5	2,447	1,245	1,202
1940	3,747	1,903	1,844	2,829	1,437	1,392	2,486	1,263	1,223
1941	3,788	1,921	1,867	2,864	1,452.5	1,411.5	2,524	1,280	1,244
1942	3,884	1,966	1,918	2,939	1,487	1,452	2,600	1,315.5	1,284.5
1943	3,915	1,982	1,933	2,962	1,498	1,464	2,629	1,329	1,300
1944	3,963	2,005	1,958	2,995	1,511.5	1,483.5	2,663	1,343.5	1,319.5
1945	4,000	2,015	1,985	3,023	1,518	1,505	2,694	1,352.5	1,341.5
1946	4,093	2,064	2,029	3,088	1,552.5	1,535.5	2,759	1,387	1,372
1947	4,176	2,106	2,070	3,135	1,575.5	1,559.5	2,808	1,410.5	1,397.5
1948	4,275	2,159	2,116	3,185	1,600	1,585	2,861	1,436.5	1,424.5
1949	4,378	2,210.5	2,167.5	3,243	1,629	1,614	2,921	1,466	1,455
1950	4,471	2,250	2,221	3,298	1,652	1,646	2,978	1,489	1,489

TABLE V–1 (continued)

	Population of all ages (in thousands)			Population of 15 years and over (in thousands)			Population of 20 years and older (in thousands)		
	Total	Male	Female	Total	Male	Female	Total	Male	Female
G. Ontario (continued)									
1951	4,598	2,314.5	2,283.5	3,358	1,680	1,678	3,043	1,520.5	1,522.5
1952	4,766	2,406	2,360	3,458	1,738	1,720	3,138	1,575	1,563
1953	4,897	2,472	2,425	3,520	1,768	1,752	3,196	1,603	1,593
1954	5,046	2,547	2,499	3,595	1,805	1,790	3,263	1,635	1,628
1955	5,183	2,615	2,568	3,656	1,834.5	1,821.5	3,316	1,660	1,656
1956	5,307	2,677	2,630	3,710	1,859.5	1,850.5	3,362	1,681	1,681
H. Manitoba									
1871	25	—	—	15	8	7	—	—	—
1872	29	—	—	17	9	8	—	—	—
1873	33	—	—	20	11	9	—	—	—
1874	37	—	—	22	12	10	—	—	—
1875	41	—	—	25	14	11	—	—	—
1876	44	—	—	27	15	12	—	—	—
1877	47	—	—	29	17	12	—	—	—
1878	50	—	—	30	18	12	—	—	—
1879	54	—	—	33	19	14	—	—	—
1880	58	—	—	35	21	14	—	—	—
1881	62	—	—	38	23	15	—	—	—
1882	71	—	—	44	27	17	—	—	—
1883	80	—	—	49	29	20	—	—	—
1884	90	—	—	55	33	22	—	—	—
1885	99	—	—	61	36	25	—	—	—
1886	108	—	—	66	39	27	—	—	—
1887	117	—	—	72	43	29	—	—	—
1888	126	—	—	77	46	31	—	—	—
1889	135	—	—	83	49	34	—	—	—
1890	144	—	—	88	52	36	—	—	—
1891	153	—	—	94	55	39	—	—	—
1892	163	—	—	100	58	42	—	—	—
1893	173	—	—	106	62	44	—	—	—

TABLE V–1 (continued)

H. Manitoba (continued)

	Population of all ages (in thousands)			Population of 15 years and over (in thousands)			Population of 20 years and older (in thousands)		
	Total	Male	Female	Total	Male	Female	Total	Male	Female
1894	183	—	—	113	65	48	—	—	—
1895	193	—	—	119	69	50	—	—	—
1896	203	—	—	125	72	53	—	—	—
1897	213	—	—	131	75	56	—	—	—
1898	223	—	—	137	78	59	—	—	—
1899	234	—	—	144	82	62	—	—	—
1900	245	—	—	151	86	65	—	—	—
1901	255	138	117	157	89	68	131	75	56
1902	275	149	126	170	96	74	143	82	61
1903	296	161	135	185	105	80	155	89	66
1904	318	173	145	200	114	86	168	97	71
1905	344	187	157	218	124	94	183	105	78
1906	366	199	167	233	133	100	197	113	84
1907	395	216	179	253	144	109	214	123	91
1908	413	226	187	266	151	115	226	130	96
1909	427	234	193	277	158	119	236	136	100
1910	441	242	199	288	164	124	246	142	104
1911	461	253	208	303	173	130	259	150	109
1912	481	263	218	315	179	136	269	155	114
1913	505	275	230	329	186	143	282	161	121
1914	530	287	243	344	193	151	295	168	127
1915	545	294	251	353	197	156	302	170	132
1916	554	298	256	357	198	159	306	172	134
1917	558	299	259	359	198	161	307	171	136
1918	565	301	264	362	198	164	310	172	138
1919	577	306	271	368	200	168	315	173	142
1920	594	314	280	377	203	174	323	176	147
1921	610	321	289	386	207	179	331	179.5	151.5
1922	616	323	293	391	209	182	335	180.5	154.5
1923	619	325	294	395	211	184	336	181	155
1924	625	327	298	400	212.5	187.5	340	182	158
1925	632	329	303	407	215	192	344	183.5	160.5

TABLE V—1 (continued)

	Population of all ages (in thousands)			Population of 15 years and over (in thousands)			Population of 20 years and older (in thousands)		
	Total	Male	Female	Total	Male	Female	Total	Male	Female
H. Manitoba (continued)									
1926	639	332	307	413	218	195	348	185	163
1927	651	339	312	426	225	201	359	191.5	167.5
1928	664	347	317	441	234	207	371	198.5	172.5
1929	677	354	323	455	242	213	383	206	177
1930	689	361.5	327.5	469	250	219	394	212	182
1931	700	368	332	481	257	224	404	218	186
1932	705	370	335	488	260	228	411	221	190
1933	708	371	337	493	262	231	417	224	193
1934	709	371	338	498	264	234	423	226.5	196.5
1935	710	371	339	503	266.5	236.5	428	229	199
1936	711	368.5	342.5	508	266	242	433	228	205
1937	715	373	342	517	273	244	442	235	207
1938	720	375	345	525	276	249	449	238	211
1939	726	378	348	533	279.5	253.5	457	241.5	215.5
1940	728	378	350	537	281	256	462	243.5	218.5
1941	730	378	352	539	281	258	465	244	221
1942	724	375.5	348.5	537	280.5	256.5	466	244.5	221.5
1943	723	375	348	537	280.5	256.5	469	246	223
1944	727	377	350	540	281.5	258.5	474	248	226
1945	727	375	352	539	280	259	475	247	228
1946	727	373	354	535	275	260	473	244	229
1947	739	378	361	542	277	265	481	246.5	234.5
1948	746	380	366	544	277	267	483	247	236
1949	757	386	371	548	279	269	489	250	239
1950	768	392	376	552	282	270	494	253	241
1951	777	395	382	554	281	273	497	252.5	244.5
1952	798	406	392	565	287	278	507	258	249
1953	809	411	398	569	288.5	280.5	512	260	252
1954	828	420	408	579	293	286	521	264	257
1955	849	430	419	589	298	291	530	268	262
1956	864	437	427	594	300	294	532	268	264

TABLE V—1 (continued)

I. Saskatchewan

Year	Population of all ages (in thousands)			Population of 15 years and over (in thousands)			Population of 20 years and older (in thousands)		
	Total	Male	Female	Total	Male	Female	Total	Male	Female
1901	91	49	42	56	31	25	47	27	20
1902	125	68	57	77	43	34	65	38	27
1903	159	87	72	99	56	43	84	49	35
1904	194	108	86	122	71	51	104	62	42
1905	236	132	104	150	88	62	127	77	50
1906	258	146	112	165	99	66	141	86	55
1907	311	177	134	200	121	79	172	106	66
1908	356	205	151	230	140	90	199	124	75
1909	401	234	167	261	162	99	226	143	83
1910	446	262	184	293	184	109	254	162	92
1911	492	292	200	325	206.5	118.5	283	183	100
1912	525	309	216	344	216	128	299	191	108
1913	563	329	234	366	228	138	318	201	117
1914	601	348	253	387	238	149	336	211	125
1915	628	361	267	401	244	157	347	215	132
1916	648	369	279	410	247	163	355	218	137
1917	662	374	288	411	245	166	359	218	141
1918	678	380	298	421	249	172	363	218	145
1919	700	389	311	431	252	179	371	220	151
1920	729	402	327	444	256	188	383	225	158
1921	758	414	344	457	261	196	393	228	165
1922	769	420	349	465	265	200	399	231	168
1923	778	424	354	472	269	203	403	233	170
1924	791	431	360	482	274	208	410	237	173
1925	806	439	367	494	281	213	418	241	177
1926	821	447	374	505	286.5	218.5	425	245	180
1927	841	457	384	524	296.5	227.5	439	253	186
1928	862	468	394	543	306.5	236.5	454	260	194
1929	883	479	404	561	316	245	468	268	200
1930	903	490	413	579	326	253	482	276	206
1931	922	500	422	595	334	261	494	283	211
1932	924	500	424	600	336	264	497	283.5	213.5

TABLE V–1 (*continued*)

I. Saskatchewan (*continued*)

	Population of all ages (in thousands)			Population of 15 years and over (in thousands)			Population of 20 years and older (in thousands)		
	Total	Male	Female	Total	Male	Female	Total	Male	Female
1933	926	501	425	606	338	268	504	287	217
1934	928	501	427	613	341	272	511	290	221
1935	930	502	428	622	345	277	520	293	227
1936	931	498	433	629	345	284	525	293	232
1937	922	495.5	426.5	629	346.5	282.5	526	294.5	231.5
1938	914	490.5	423.5	628	345	283	526	293.5	232.5
1939	906	485	421	627	343	284	526	292	234
1940	900	481	419	628	342.5	285.5	528	292	236
1941	896	478	418	628	341.5	286.5	532	293	239
1942	848	455.5	392.5	597	328	269	507	282	225
1943	838	451	387	595	327	268	506	281	225
1944	836	449	387	596	326.5	269.5	509	282	227
1945	833	447	386	595	325	270	511	281.5	229.5
1946	833	442	391	592	319.5	272.5	511	278	233
1947	836	443	393	593	319	274	514	279	235
1948	838	445	393	592	319	273	515	279.5	235.5
1949	832	437	395	584	311.5	272.5	510	273.5	236.5
1950	833	437	396	581	309	272	510	273	237
1951	832	435	397	576	304	272	508	270	238
1952	843	439	404	583	307	276	514	272	242
1953	861	448	413	593	312	281	524	277	247
1954	878	457	421	600	316	284	532	281.5	250.5
1955	889	462	427	605	317	288	536	282	254
1956	897	464	433	610	319	291	541	284	257

J. Alberta

	Total	Male	Female	Total	Male	Female	Total	Male	Female
1901	73	41	32	45	26.5	18.5	39	23	16
1902	96	54	42	60	36	24	52	31	21
1903	119	68	51	75	45	30	65	39	26
1904	142	81	61	90	58	32	78	47	31
1905	166	96	70	106	65	41	93	57	36

TABLE V—1 (continued)

	Population of all ages (in thousands)			Population of 15 years and over (in thousands)			Population of 20 years and older (in thousands)		
	Total	Male	Female	Total	Male	Female	Total	Male	Female

J. Alberta (continued)

	Total	Male	Female	Total	Male	Female	Total	Male	Female
1906	185	107	78	120	74	46	104	64	40
1907	236	138	98	154	95	59	134	84	50
1908	266	156	110	175	109	66	153	97	56
1909	301	178	123	200	126	74	175	111	64
1910	336	200	136	225	143	82	197	116	81
1911	374	223.5	150.5	253	161.5	91.5	222	144	78
1912	400	237	163	269	170	99	236	152	84
1913	429	252	177	287	180	107	251	159	92
1914	459	268	191	305	189	116	267	168	99
1915	480	278	202	317	194	123	277	172	105
1916	496	285	211	326	198	128	285	175	110
1917	508	289	219	332	200	132	290	177	113
1918	522	295	227	339	202	137	296	178	118
1919	541	303	238	349	205	144	304	181	123
1920	565	314	251	363	211	152	315	186	129
1921	589	324.5	264.5	375	216	159	326	190	136
1922	592	325.5	266.5	377	216	161	327	190	137
1923	593	326	267	379	217	162	328	190	138
1924	597	327	270	382	218	164	329	190.5	138.5
1925	602	329	273	387	220	167	332	192	140
1926	608	331	277	392	222.5	169.5	335	193	142
1927	633	345	288	411	233	178	351	202	149
1928	658	359	299	432	245	187	368	212	156
1929	684	374	310	454	257.5	196.5	386	222.5	163.5
1930	708	387	321	474	269	205	403	233	170
1931	732	400.5	331.5	493	279.5	213.5	419	242	177
1932	740	404	336	500	282.5	217.5	425	244.5	180.5
1933	750	409	341	510	287.5	222.5	435	249	186
1934	758	412	346	520	292	228	444	253	191
1935	765	415.5	349.5	529	296	233	453	257.5	195.5
1936	773	418	355	536	298.5	237.5	458	259	199
1937	776	420	356	546	304	242	467	263	204

TABLE V—1 (continued)

	Population of all ages (in thousands)			Population of 15 years and over (in thousands)			Population of 20 years and older (in thousands)		
	Total	Male	Female	Total	Male	Female	Total	Male	Female

J. Alberta (continued)

	Total	Male	Female	Total	Male	Female	Total	Male	Female
1938	781	421.5	359.5	553	306	247	472	265	207
1939	786	423	363	558	308	250	478	267.5	210.5
1940	790	424	366	563	309.5	253.5	483	269	214
1941	796	426.5	369.5	568	311	257	490	272	218
1942	776	417	359	555	305	250	480	267.5	212.5
1943	785	421	364	563	308.5	254.5	489	271	218
1944	808	432	376	580	316	264	506	278.5	227.5
1945	808	429	379	579	313	266	506	276.5	229.5
1946	803	424	379	573	307	266	501	271	230
1947	825	435	390	584	312	272	512	276	236
1948	854	448	406	601	320	281	529	284	245
1949	885	464	421	621	331	290	548	293.5	254.5
1950	913	479	434	637	339	298	564	301.5	262.5
1951	940	492.5	447.5	653	346.5	306.5	579	308.5	270.5
1952	970	508.5	461.5	669	355	314	595	316.5	278.5
1953	1,002	524	478	685	362	323	610	323.5	286.5
1954	1,039	542.5	496.5	703	371	332	626	331.5	294.5
1955	1,066	556	510	714	376	338	636	336	300
1956	1,092	569	523	724	381	343	645	340	305

K. British Columbia

	Total	Male	Female	Total	Male	Female	Total	Male	Female
1871	36	—	—	25	15	10	—	—	—
1872	37	—	—	26	16	10	—	—	—
1873	39	—	—	27	16	11	—	—	—
1874	40	—	—	28	17	11	—	—	—
1875	42	—	—	29	18	11	—	—	—
1876	43	—	—	30	18	12	—	—	—
1877	44	—	—	31	19	12	—	—	—
1878	45	—	—	32	20	12	—	—	—
1879	46	—	—	33	21	12	—	—	—

TABLE V–1 (continued)

K. British Columbia (continued)

Year	Population of all ages (in thousands)			Population of 15 years and over (in thousands)			Population of 20 years and older (in thousands)		
	Total	Male	Female	Total	Male	Female	Total	Male	Female
1880	48	—	—	34	21	13	—	—	—
1881	49	—	—	35	22	13	—	—	—
1882	54	—	—	39	25	14	—	—	—
1883	59	—	—	43	28	15	—	—	—
1884	64	—	—	46	30	16	—	—	—
1885	69	—	—	50	33	17	—	—	—
1886	74	—	—	54	35	19	—	—	—
1887	78	—	—	57	38	19	—	—	—
1888	83	—	—	61	41	20	—	—	—
1889	88	—	—	65	44	21	—	—	—
1890	93	—	—	69	47	22	—	—	—
1891	98	—	—	73	50	23	—	—	—
1892	106	—	—	79	54	25	—	—	—
1893	114	—	—	85	58	27	—	—	—
1894	122	—	—	91	62	29	—	—	—
1895	130	—	—	97	66	31	—	—	—
1896	138	—	—	103	70	33	—	—	—
1897	146	—	—	109	74	35	—	—	—
1898	154	—	—	115	78	37	—	—	—
1899	162	—	—	121	82	39	—	—	—
1900	170	—	—	127	86	41	—	—	—
1901	179	114	65	134	91	43	121	84	37
1902	199	127	72	149	101	48	135	94	41
1903	220	140	80	165	112	53	150	104	46
1904	242	154	88	182	124	58	165	115	50
1905	264	169	95	199	135	64	181	126	55
1906	279	178	101	211	144	67	192	133	59
1907	309	198	111	235	160	75	213	148	65
1908	330	211	119	251	171	80	228	158	70
1909	350	224	126	267	182	85	243	169	74
1910	370	237	133	283	193	90	257	178	79

TABLE V—1 (continued)

K. British Columbia (continued)

	Population of all ages (in thousands)			Population of 15 years and over (in thousands)			Population of 20 years and older (in thousands)		
	Total	Male	Female	Total	Male	Female	Total	Male	Female
1911	393	252	141	301	205	96	274	190	84
1912	407	258	149	310	208	102	282	193	89
1913	424	265	159	320	212	108	291	196	95
1914	442	273	169	332	215	117	301	199	102
1915	450	274	176	335	215	120	304	198	106
1916	456	274	182	338	213	125	306	196	110
1917	464	275	189	341	212	129	309	195	114
1918	474	277	197	346	211	135	313	194	119
1919	488	281	207	354	213	141	319	195	124
1920	507	288	219	365	216	149	329	197	132
1921	525	293.5	231.5	375	218	157	338	199	139
1922	541	301	240	390	225	165	350	205	145
1923	555	308	247	402	230	172	361	209.5	151.5
1924	571	315	256	416	236	180	372	214	158
1925	588	323	265	432	244	188	385	220	165
1926	606	332	274	447	252	195	398	227	171
1927	623	342	281	462	260.5	201.5	410	234.5	175.5
1928	641	353.5	287.5	477	270	207	423	243	180
1929	659	364	295	492	279.5	212.5	436	251	185
1930	676	374	302	507	289	218	448	259	189
1931	694	385	309	523	298.5	224.5	461	267	194
1932	707	390	317	536	304	232	472	271.5	200.5
1933	717	395	322	547	308.5	238.5	485	277	208

TABLE V—1 (continued)

K. British Columbia (continued)

	Population of all ages (in thousands)			Population of 15 years and over (in thousands)			Population of 20 years and older (in thousands)		
	Total	Male	Female	Total	Male	Female	Total	Male	Female
1934	727	399	328	558	313	245	497	282	215
1935	736	402	334	570	318	252	509	287	222
1936	745	407.5	337.5	586	326.5	259.5	525	296	229
1937	759	412	347	596	329	267	532	297	235
1938	775	418	357	610	334.5	275.5	544	301	243
1939	792	425	367	624	340	284	556	305.5	250.5
1940	805	430	375	635	344	291	567	309.5	257.5
1941	818	435	383	643	346.5	296.5	576	312.5	263.5
1942	870	458.5	411.5	681	363	318	613	329	284
1943	900	472	428	701	371	330	633	337	296
1944	932	486	446	722	379.5	342.5	653	345	308
1945	949	491.5	457.5	733	383	350	663	348	315
1946	1,003	522	481	771	403.5	367.5	700	368	332
1947	1,044	542	502	796	415.5	380.5	724	380	344
1948	1,082	562.5	519.5	821	430	391	749	393	356
1949	1,113	575	538	837	435	402	765	398	367
1950	1,137	584	553	849	438	411	777	401.5	375.5
1951	1,165	597	568	861	442	419	791	406.5	384.5
1952	1,198	613	585	877	450	427	805	413	392
1953	1,230	628	602	891	455	436	817	417	400
1954	1,266	646	620	910	464	446	832	424	408
1955	1,305	664	641	929	472	457	848	431	417
1956	1,353	686	667	953	481	472	867	437.5	429.5

SOURCES AND NOTES

Table V—1, A-K

The following sources of population data were utilized.

1921-1956. All figures, for both census and intercensal years, were based on data provided in *Population Estimates (Age and Sex), 1921-1952* (Ottawa: Dominion Bureau of Statistics), Reference Paper No. 40, 1953 (with supplementary tabulations 1953-1956).

1871-1920. Figures for the total population only, in both census and intercensal years, were obtained from the *Eighth Census of Canada* (Ottawa: D.B.S.), I, p. 1027.

1881-1911. The sex breakdown of total population, and the population of 15 years and older, and of 20 years and older, by sex, where shown for the census years 1881, 1891, 1901 and 1911, were obtained from the *Ninth Census of Canada* (Ottawa: D.B.S.), X, Table 8.

1871. Figures for the population of 15 years and older, by sex, in Nova Scotia, New Brunswick, Ontario, and Quebec were obtained from the *First Census of Canada*, V, Table F. Such data were not available for Prince Edward Island, Manitoba, and British Columbia. The figures shown for these provinces represent estimates obtained in the following manner. The proportion of persons 15 years and older in the total population of each sex in 1881 was calculated for each of the three provinces. The resulting proportions were then applied to the appropriate 1871 totals, by sex, provided in the *Ninth Census of Canada*, I, Table 16. Judging by all available trend data, the estimates obtained in this manner probably do not differ from the true figures by more than 5 percent. The figures for the population of 15 years and older, by sex, shown for Canada, represent the sum of provincial data.

The method employed to estimate all figures other than those noted above is most easily explained by reference to a specific case, for example, the derivation of the estimates of population 20 years and older in British Columbia for the intercensal period 1912 to 1920. The total population of British Columbia in the census year 1911 was approximately 393,000, and that of 20 years and older, 274,000 or 69.72 percent of the total. In the census year 1921, the population of 20 years and older comprised 64.38 percent of the total. On the assumption that the change in proportion over the intercensal period had been arithmetic in nature, the absolute difference (5.34) was divided by 10, and the result (0.534) successively subtracted from 69.72 to obtain a series of nine proportions. Each of these was then applied to the appropriate intercensal estimate of total population obtained from the *Eighth Census* (see above). To obtain estimates of the male population of 20 years and older, the same procedure was followed. Specifically, the proportion of males in the total population of 20 years and older was calculated for each census year, the absolute difference divided by 10, and the result successively subtracted from the proportion in 1911 (since this proportion was the larger of the two). The series of proportions were then applied to corresponding estimates of the total population of 20 years and older previously derived. Estimates of the female population were obtained by subtraction.

This method was employed to derive the sex breakdown of total population for the intercensal years between 1901 and 1921, the population of 15 years and older by sex for the intercensal years between 1871 and 1921, and the population of 20 years and older by sex for the intercensal years between 1901 and 1921. Other relatively more laborious and complex methods of intercensal estimation—for

154

example, those employing logarithmic functions or successive integration—may have provided better approximations. However, a few trials suggested that differences in results would ordinarily be very small, and unlikely appreciably to affect the various rates based on these figures.

All figures shown for Canada are exclusive of the Yukon and Northwest Territories throughout, and of Newfoundland until 1949. Parenthetically, Alberta and Saskatchewan were part of the Northwest Territories until 1901. The small discrepancies encountered in certain years between the figures for Canada and the sum of provincial figures represent rounding errors.